Community Organizing

Social Movements series

Stephanie Luce, *Labor Movements: Global Perspectives*

David Walls, *Community Organizing: Fanning the Flame of Democracy*

Community Organizing

Fanning the Flame of Democracy

David Walls

polity

First published in 2015 by Polity Press
Reprinted 2017(twice)

Polity Press
65 Bridge Street
Cambridge CB2 1UR, UK

Polity Press
350 Main Street
Malden, MA 02148, USA

ISBN-13: 978-0-7456-6319-7
ISBN-13: 978-0-7456-6320-3 (pb)

A catalogue record for this book is available from the British Library.

Typeset in 11 on 13 pt Sabon by
Servis Filmsetting Ltd, Stockport, Cheshire
Printed and bound in the United States by LSC Communications

The publisher has used its best endeavours to ensure that the URLs for external websites referred to in this book are correct and active at the time of going to press. However, the publisher has no responsibility for the websites and can make no guarantee that a site will remain live or that the content is or will remain appropriate.

Every effort has been made to trace all copyright holders, but if any have been inadvertently overlooked the publisher will be pleased to include any necessary credits in any subsequent reprint or edition.

For further information on Polity, visit our website: politybooks.com

Contents

Abbreviations

AALC   African American Leadership Commission
ABCD   asset-based community development
ACORN   Association of Community Organizations for Reform Now
ACT   Allied Communities of Tarrant
AFL   American Federation of Labor
BUILD   Baltimoreans United in Leadership Development
BYNC   Back of the Yards Neighborhood Council
CBA   community benefit agreement
CBCO   congregation-based community organization
(C)CHD   (Catholic) Campaign for Human Development
CDBG   Community Development Block Grant
CDGM   Child Development Group of Mississippi
CIO   Committee on Industrial Organization
CO   council organizer
COPS   Communities Organized for Public Service
CORE   Congress of Racial Equality
CP   Communist Party
CSO   Community Service Organization
CWA   Communication Workers of America
DART   Direct Action and Research Training Center
EBC   East Brooklyn Congregations
ERAP   Economic Research and Action Project
FIGHT   Freedom, Integration, God, Honor, Today
IAF   Industrial Areas Foundation

IBCO	institution-based community organization
IJR	Institute for Juvenile Research
IMF	International Monetary Fund
IVE	integrated voter engagement
JwJ	Jobs with Justice
LULAC	League of United Latin American Citizens
NAACP	National Association for the Advancement of Colored People
NBOP	North Bay Organizing Project
NIRA	National Industrial Recovery Act
NPA	National People's Action
NTIC	National Training and Information Center
OBA	Organization for a Better Austin
OEO	Office of Economic Opportunity
OFA	Obama for America/Organizing for America/ Organizing for Action
OSR	Occupy Santa Rosa
OWS	Occupy Wall Street
PICO	Pacific Institute for Community Organization/ People Improving Communities through Organizing
PNCC	Pilsen Neighbors Community Council
PWOC	Packinghouse Workers Organizing Committee
RO	regional organizer
SCLC	Southern Christian Leadership Conference
SDS	Students for a Democratic Society
SMART	Sonoma–Marin Area Rail Transit
SMI	social movement industry
SMO	social movement organization
SNCC	Student Nonviolent Coordinating Committee
SPIN	Segmented Polycentric Ideological Networks
TEN	Transportation Equity Network
TMO	The Metropolitan Organization
TWO	The Woodlawn Organization
UFW	United Farm Workers

Abbreviations

UMWA	United Mine Workers of America
USCC	United States Catholic Conference
WTO	World Trade Organization
WUNC	worthiness, unity, numbers, and commitment

1

Introduction: Making Change

Is the world to be changed? How? By whom?
The skeptical "first god" in
The Good Person of Szechwan
by Bertolt Brecht

Can the world be changed? Bertolt Brecht's challenging question continues to provoke. Community organizers answer with a resounding "Yes!" But exactly how? And who would be the active agents of change?

This book argues that the tradition of community organizing launched by Saul Alinsky, as modified and developed, offers concepts and tools that are indispensable to a democratic strategy of social change that promotes grassroots leadership and power for social, economic, racial, and environmental justice. Some critics have claimed the scale of community organizing is too small for the task of making transformative change in a large and complex society. But it's no longer just about stop signs, block clubs, and neighborhood associations. Consistent with Alinsky's original vision, the scope of community organizing has expanded to include cities, metropolitan areas, states, and even national government policy. Alinsky's approach to organizing, like the man himself, was a product of his time and place, and needed to be modified to thrive in changing circumstances. We will look at the development of this organizing tradition through a framework of social movement analysis, assess its strengths and weaknesses, and

1

examine proposals to modify and develop community organizing to meet its promise of deepening democracy in our challenging times of expanding inequality.

This introductory chapter will define community organizing and social movements, glance at recent controversies about community organizing in national political races, present a typology that distinguishes community organizing from many other examples of social movements, and examine how community organizing figured in twentieth-century social reform. Chapter 2 explores the social, political, and intellectual forces that influenced Alinsky from the 1930s to the 1960s. Following Alinsky's death in 1972, the Industrial Areas Foundation (IAF) under Ed Chambers began to systematize the training and practice of community organizing. The approach developed by Chambers and Ernesto Cortes, Jr. in the 1970s – a very different time from Alinsky's – focused on developing an organization whose members are primarily religious congregations – often termed congregation-based community organizations (CBCOs). Today this approach is itself 40 years old and in need of updating. We will examine the innovations Chambers, Cortes, and others introduced to the IAF, and begin to assess whether they still match the circumstances of our time.

The IAF training programs, launched by Alinsky but developed and standardized by Chambers, have created an organizing culture that brings staff organizers and community leaders together in long-range commitments to one another and to the community organizing process. Chapter 3 outlines the essential features of the Alinsky tradition's distinctive organizing worldview, which has had much to do with the success of CBCOs.

Chapter 4 surveys the "tools of the trade" of community organizing, many of which have been borrowed to one degree or another by movement organizations not necessarily sharing the worldview or organizational culture of the networks in the Alinsky tradition.

A venerable tool of community organizations in the Alinsky tradition is the public meeting, or accountability session, often an organization's annual highlight gathering. Rather than simply analyze the elements of these pieces of public theater, Chapter 4 features a case study of the first public meeting, in October 2011, of the North Bay Organizing Project in California. The study tries to communicate a sense of the excitement that can occur at such events when there are genuine victories won that deserve celebration.

Chapter 5 explores the development of some distinctive contributions made by other new networks of community organizations. Of particular interest are the national networks – PICO, Gamaliel, National People's Action, and ACORN – as they began to influence policy at the national level. Virginia Hine's SPIN model of network analysis, which we will examine in that chapter, explains the ability of the network form to protect organizations from internal scandal and external attack.

The community organizing approach has been modified to apply to political campaigns, online activism, and mainstream social movement groups. Most notable is the work of Marshall Ganz, who worked with Cesar Chavez and the United Farm Workers (UFW) for many years, served as a political consultant for Democrats from Nancy Pelosi to Barack Obama, and now teaches at Harvard University's Kennedy School of Government. Chapter 6 looks at the applications of his approach. Chapter 7 examines other alternatives to the Alinsky tradition, including the popular education work of the Highlander Center, and the efforts to reduce hierarchy in organizational structure that fit under the title of horizontalism – ranging from the participatory democracy of the 1960s New Left, radical feminist groups, anti-nuclear and anti-globalization movements, and the recent Occupy movement. Finally, Chapter 8 considers various critiques of the community organizing tradition, and proposals to increase its power to win structural reforms and transformational change on a national level, particularly in alliance with labor and other social movements.

Barack Obama: The First Organizer President

Barack Obama's successful 2008 Presidential campaign drew attention to community organizing by highlighting his work as an organizer in Chicago from 1985 to 1988, between completing his undergraduate studies at Columbia University and his decision to attend Harvard Law School. Obama had worked in far-south Chicago with the Developing Communities Project associated with the Gamaliel Foundation, a network of community organizing projects in the Alinsky tradition (Obama 1995: 133–86). He was mentored by Jerry Kellman and Mike Kruglik of the Gamaliel staff.

Conservative critics were vocal. In her Vice-Presidential candidate acceptance speech at the 2008 Republican convention, Alaska governor Sarah Palin commented sarcastically, "I guess a small-town mayor is sort of like a 'community organizer,' except that you have actual responsibilities" (Katz 2008–9). Campaigning in the 2012 Republican primary, former Congressman and House majority leader Newt Gingrich asserted, "The centerpiece of this campaign is American exceptionalism versus the radicalism of Saul Alinsky."

Hard-right author David Horowitz used the writings of Alinsky to attack Obama in his polemical pamphlet *Barack Obama's Rules for Revolution: The Alinsky Model* (Horowitz 2009), then promoted tactics similar to those he ascribed to Alinsky in another pamphlet, *The Art of Political War for Tea Parties* (Horowitz 2010). Some conservatives seemed obsessed with finding deeper connections between Alinsky and President Obama, despite the fact that Alinsky died in 1972 when Obama was 10 years old, and – no surprise – they never met.

The irony in this story is that Obama had come to doubt the efficacy of the Alinsky community organizing approach to make the changes in society that he had hoped to foster. In his 1988 article in *Illinois Issues*, "Why Organize? Problems and Promise in the Inner City," reprinted in *After Alinsky* (Obama 1990), Obama noted the contending alternative strategies of political empowerment, economic development, and grassroots organizing. He cited the economic self-help approach of Northwestern University professor John McKnight (see Chapter 7) as one promising supplement to community organizing. Although Obama remained upbeat in this article, it is clear he was becoming disillusioned with what he could accomplish working as a community organizer. In a round-table discussion in September 1989 on "Organizing in the 1990s," among the authors of the articles collected in *After Alinsky*, Obama draws a sharper critique of the Alinsky tradition. First, organizing needs to place more emphasis on its long-term vision, based on its values, and less emphasis on people's short-term self-interest. Second, Alinsky's criticism of charismatic leaders and social movements, taken up especially by the IAF under Chambers, has been carried too far. And finally, avoidance of direct political involvement is a mistake; in the end politics is essential to obtaining the power to make social changes that can impact low-income communities across the country (Knoepfle 1990: 132–4). As we know, after completing law school Obama entered elective politics, running campaigns that built on his skills as a charismatic speaker and that had some of the feel of a social movement. John Judis may have exaggerated when he argued that Obama's choice of a political career was more a "wholesale rejection" than an embrace of community organizing in the Alinsky tradition (Judis 2008: 19), but it is clear Obama personally had decided to approach making change from a different direction. The use of some organizing techniques in the Presidential campaign does not make it an example of good community organizing practice (Stout 2010: 260–77).

Community Organizing

By and large, community organizers welcomed the attention the Obama campaign brought to their profession, absurd and distorted as the references often were (Dreier and Moberg 2008–9). More young people were attracted to careers as organizers (Rimer 2009), and more communities were moved to develop broad-based community organizations. Whether these trends continue or not, community organizing has a higher public profile than it did before Obama's Presidency.

There has been a substantial expansion of institution-based community organizations (IBCOs) over the last 20 years, especially in the last decade, mostly taking place under the radar of the mass media. As of 2011, a comprehensive study of the field by Interfaith Funders identified 189 active IBCOs operating in 40 states. The 178 IBCOs that responded to the survey had some 4,100 member institutions, primarily religious congregations, which represent some 5 million people (Wood et al. 2013: ii–iv). That's an increase from approximately 133 groups in 1999 and more than double the number of some 90 groups in 1994. Congregation-based community organizing has become a significant expression of religious traditions of working for social justice (Slessarev-Jamir 2011: 67–96). But this success contains a puzzle. Community organizing is, at best, known locally; the major national networks have little national visibility. Political scientist Peter Dreier has caught this paradox in noting that "the whole of the community organizing movement is smaller than the sum of its parts" (Dreier 2007: 221). Why this may be so, and how organizers and leaders can realize the full potential of this movement, we will address over the course of this book.

What exactly is community organizing? Let's begin with a broad definition from Doran Schrantz, executive director of ISAIAH, an organization of over 100 congregations in the St. Paul–Minneapolis area: "Organizing is a set of strategic disciplines and practices to build the capacity of people to participate in and shape democratic life" (Schrantz 2013). I would add a somewhat more detailed definition:

> Community organizing is a process that seeks to build powerful, purposeful, coordinated, and disciplined activity by groups of people who support and challenge each other to affirm, defend and advance their values and self-interests. (Adapted from Mike Miller 1987)

This definition serves to emphasize that participants are serious about building powerful organizations, based on their interests and values, in which they are accountable to one another for their contributions toward the common goals.

The 2013 study by Interfaith Funders drew the following conclusion:

Collectively, IBCOs represent a social movement dedicated to building democratic power, strengthening public life, and improving social
conditions in low-income and working-class communities. . . . They
bolster public life by identifying leaders and developing them into
effective advocates for their communities. In doing so, they help
communities organize and generate power that can be channeled
toward shaping public policy to meet needs at the local level and,
increasingly, at the state and national level as well. (Wood et al.
2013: 3)

Social Movements

A premise of this book is that the field of community organizing
can be considered as a type of social movement, and can be illu-
minated by applying social movement analysis. My definition of
"social movement" is a composite drawing on several theorists
who develop insights from the disciplines of sociology, political
science, and history:

> Collective efforts, on the part of people and organizations with
> common purposes, to promote or resist changes in the culture or struc-
> ture of society that often use non-institutional methods in sustained
> interaction, sometimes over years and decades, with elites, opponents,
> and authorities (Flacks 2005: 5; McAdam 1982: 25; Moyer 2001: 2;
> Tarrow 1994: 1). Participants often make "public representations of
> worthiness, unity, numbers, and commitment (WUNC)" (Tilly 2004:
> 3–4).

Here movements are distinguished from interest groups through
their willingness to use non-institutional methods – direct action,
demonstrations, boycotts, sit-ins, and the like – beyond the usual
lobbying of officials in the executive or legislative branches of
government or executives of private corporations, or taking legal
action through the court system.

Community Organizing as a Social Movement

The claim that community organizing can be considered a social movement is controversial, as leaders of the networks in the Alinsky tradition – particularly the IAF under Chambers – have argued that community organizing has little in common with social movements, and have criticized several features they see as characteristic of such movements. Political scientist Heidi Swarts presents a typology in her 2008 book *Organizing Urban America* that can reconcile these seemingly opposite positions. She develops two ideal types (as the term is used by Max Weber), which she labels "A" and "B," but which have more intuitive meaning if we designate them "Protest Movements" and "Strategic Movements" (with community organizing being an example of a Strategic Movement) (see Table 1.1).

"Strategic" in this context means having a method and plan to achieve a specific objective. The two ideal types lie at the extremes of a continuum connecting the pair of opposites, such as instrumental (Strategic) to expressive (Protest). Few movements represent either of the pure types. As Swarts notes, "actual social movements combine elements of both types" (Swarts 2008: xxvii).

Table 1.1 Two ideal types of social movements

Strategic Movements	Protest Movements
Instrumental	Expressive
Power	Virtue
Winning	Speaking truth to power
Self-interest	Altruism
Negotiation and compromise	Purity
Hierarchical	Horizontalist
Distributed leadership	Charismatic leadership
Majority vote	Consensus
Electoral politics	Direct action
Ongoing	Episodic
Weber's ethic of responsibility	Weber's ethic of ultimate ends

Source: Adapted from Swarts 2008: xxviii.

Nevertheless, identifying the two ideal types by their extremes clarifies their differences. Strategic Movements accept compromise through negotiation; Protest Movements favor purity. Strategic Movements are ongoing; Protest Movements are generally episodic. Protest Movements tend to be egalitarian, with decisions made by consensus; Strategic Movements tend to be hierarchical with decisions made by majority vote. Protest Movements distrust and avoid elective politics; Strategic Movements distrust but embrace politics (Swarts 2008: xxvii–xxx). Examples of Protest Movements include Prohibition, the radical peace movement, women's liberation, and animal rights. Strategic Movements include the labor movement as well as community organizing (not surprising in light of the close ties between labor and Saul Alinsky, as Chapter 2 will show), as well as mainstream elements of the peace, environmental, women's, and humane movements.

Social Movement Analysis

Schools of social movement analysis with the greatest application to the study of community organizing include resource mobilization, political process and opportunity, social constructionism, and the recent "new social movements" approaches. The classical "collective behavior" approach would appear to be less useful, for reasons developed below.

Collective Behavior

The contemporary schools of analysis emerged from the study of the social movements of the 1960s. Until the 1970s, the field defined itself primarily as the study of "collective behavior." This classical explanation of social movements focused on such phenomena as crowds, crazes, cults, mobs, riots, fads, panics, and financial bubbles. Irrational behavior was emphasized by such early works as Charles Mackay's *Extraordinary Popular Delusions and the Madness of Crowds* (1841) and Gustave Le Bon's *The Crowd* (1895). In this view, industrialization, urbanization, and rapid population growth disrupt and break down traditional social life, creating strain in individuals, resulting in alienation, anomie, a sense of relative deprivation, and unmet expectations. A popular critique of mass movements by Eric Hoffer, *The True Believer* (1951), was widely read in the 1950s and early 1960s. Writing in the wake of the Second World War, Hoffer emphasized the irrational elements of fascism, Nazism, and communism as well as religious fanaticism (Buechler 2004). The exceptions to the focus on the irrationality of movement participants were studies of the labor and socialist movements by writers sympathetic to their objectives (see Laidler 1944), often influenced by Marxism or other forms of structural analysis.

Resource Mobilization

The civil rights movement of the late 1950s and 1960s began to erode the appeal of collective behavior theory. Civil rights activists didn't appear irrational in seeking equal rights under the law. Demonstrators seemed disciplined, courageous, principled in their practice of nonviolence, and rational in their demands. A new emphasis on organization, members, and money emerged, known as resource mobilization theory, identified most strongly with Mayer Zald and his students and colleagues (see Zald and McCarthy 1987). As Steven Buechler writes, resource mobilization understands that social movements consist of "rational actors engaged in instrumental action through formal organization to secure resources and foster mobilization" (Buechler 1995: 441). In the civil rights movement in the South, for example, sociologist Aldon Morris (1984) showed that African Americans organized branches of the National Association for the Advancement of Colored People (NAACP) in their communities, ministers organized the Southern Christian Leadership Conference (SCLC) to bring together the churches, and students at historically black colleges organized into chapters of SNCC, the Student Nonviolent Coordinating Committee.

When community organizers point out that power has two sources, organized people and organized money, they are speaking from a resource mobilization perspective (whether they realize it or not). Resource mobilization theory distinguishes between social movements and social movement organizations (SMOs), viewed as the crucial vehicles for social movements. Within a given social movement, the SMOs together constitute a social movement industry, to use an economic metaphor, and can be expected to compete for resources, including members and money, as well as to cooperate (Zald and McCarthy 1987). Social movements thus have multi-organizational fields, including all those organizations movements may interact with, both supportive and antagonistic. Allies and opponents may include political parties, religious congregations, labor unions, advocacy groups, and others (Rucht 2004).

Resource mobilization also points out that external sources of funds, including foundations and government, are increasingly important for contemporary SMOs. Community organizing in the Alinsky tradition emphasizes the independence that results from achieving self-support through membership dues and grassroots fundraising. Foundation grants have nevertheless been important to community organizing, with the Catholic Campaign for Human Development being a leading supporter of congregation-based community organizing. The increasing professionalization of social reform is also highlighted (McCarthy and Zald 1973). Resource mobilization theory helps explain the dynamics of the national community organizing networks described in Chapters 2 and 5.

Political Process and Opportunity

Political process extends resource mobilization theory to account for changes in the political sphere. The political process school (also known as the political opportunity structure approach) analyzes the impact of shifts in political power and structure on the cost of challenging authorities. The capacity or the will of authorities to repress mobilizing may shift over time, making the cost/benefit calculation for such mobilization more or less attractive. "Windows of political opportunity" may open or close depending on which person or party wins an election, on redistricting, or on changes in the method of elections (e.g. from at-large to district elections for a city council). Factionalism within a governing elite can also provide a "window of opportunity" for an insurgent group (Tarrow 1994: 81–99). This process takes place on the municipal level as well as in state and national politics, as historian J. Mills Thornton III (2002) has shown in his analysis of the civil rights movement in three Alabama cities: Montgomery, Birmingham, and Selma. The analysis of political opportunities is an element in the power analysis that community organizations should complete as they strategize issues being considered for action.

Social Constructionism

Social constructionist theories look at the active human subject creating the social world, acting upon the world rather than being shaped by it, as in structural theories. The analysis of "framing" activity is an important element of this school of thought (Snow 2004). Movement cycles often emerge with the development of a compelling "master frame," as the civil rights movement did with the "equal rights" frame. Subsequent movements such as the women's movement, the gay and lesbian movement, the disability movement, and even the animal rights movement have derived their own collective action frames from the master frame of "equal rights" developed by the civil rights movement (Snow and Benford 1992). The creation of new collective identities is a social construction that is often part of a movement's work. We get a deeper insight into the perspectives, tools, tactics, and skills taught by the community organizing networks when we see how they help construct new identities for organizers, leaders, and active members of community groups. This perspective on framing will be helpful in understanding the worldviews and organizing tools imparted in the networks' training programs discussed in Chapter 3.

New Social Movements

A notable feature of many social movements emerging during the 1960s and 1970s was their emphasis on subculture and identity, rather than class (as in the "old" social movements of labor and the socialist left). Black Power, women's liberation, and Queer Nation are all examples of a new emphasis on race, gender, or sexual orientation as the focus of activist identity. Proponents argue that new social movements are "a product of the shift to a postindustrial economy," and are fundamentally different from prior industrial-era movements. They generally avoid the political arena, and form organizations that minimize hierarchy and seek consensus. Activists are drawn primarily from the "new" middle class (Pichardo 1997: 411–17). As this emphasis is less characteristic of community organizing, generally speaking, we can understand identity and subculture from the perspective of social constructionist theory, as described above. But if we view the decline of civic associations as a result of modern society's tendency to produce alienation and isolation of individuals, the "horizontalist fringe" of the community organizing movement could be seen as one of the resulting new social movements.

Waves of Reform and the Emergence of Community Organizing

Students of social movements have long noted the apparent tendency for social reforms in the United States to take place in waves. Historian Arthur Schlesinger, Jr. (1986) saw 30-year cycles in which social policy swung from public purpose to private interest and back again. The Populist and Progressive Eras, the New Deal, and the Great Society are four significant reform periods that continue to be discussed in histories of community organizing. Social movements typically provide a dynamic that drives reform, often to partial rather than complete success of movement goals. Problems of disparities of income and wealth; persistence of poverty; racism and the denial of civil rights; integration of immigrants; rights of labor; industrialization and urban life; public education for civic life and work skills; health care for all; income support in retirement and old age – all are themes from earlier eras that continue to be reflected in the issues of community organizing today.

Populism

Harry Boyte, one of the first activist-academics to study and write extensively on community organizing (see Boyte 1980, 1984, 1989; Boyte and Riessman 1986; Boyte et al. 1986), character izes community organizing as "the new Populism." The historic Populist movement in the United States was embodied in the Farmers' Alliance, first formed in 1877, and the People's Party, founded in 1891. An agrarian movement, Populism was strongest among cotton farmers in the South and wheat farmers in the Great Plains. The movement had considerable impact on the election of 1892, when the People's Party ran James Weaver for President on a platform that called for an eight-hour working day, a graduated income tax, direct election of Senators, government ownership of railroads, civil service reform, and abolition of national banks.

In 1896 the People's Party supported William Jennings Bryan, the Democratic candidate for President, on a fusion ticket (meaning a vote could be cast for Bryan either on the Democratic line or the Populist line). Bryan discarded most of the Populists' "Omaha Platform" of 1892, but did emphasize his opposition to the gold standard and support for free coinage of silver, a strategy that would lead to monetary inflation, allowing farmers to repay their debts with cheaper money. At the Democratic National Convention in July 1896, Bryan delivered his famous "cross of gold" speech, which concluded with the memorable lines, "You shall not press down upon the brow of labor this crown of thorns; you shall not crucify mankind upon a cross of gold." After Bryan's loss to Republican William McKinley, the Populist movement declined sharply, and the People's Party collapsed (Hicks 1931). One Populist Era reform that survives today is the Bank of North Dakota, which serves as a model of what a state-owned bank could do for community economic development. Historian Lawrence Goodwyn summarized the dilemma of the Populists: "the practical shortcoming of the Populist political effort was one the agrarian reformers did not fully comprehend: their attempts to construct a national farmer–labor coalition came before the fledgling American labor movement was internally prepared for mass insurgent politics" (Goodwyn 1978: 297).

Michael Kazin, a contemporary historian of the movement, defines populism as more a rhetoric than an ideology: "a language whose speakers conceive of ordinary people as a noble assemblage not narrowly bounded by class, view their elite opponents as self-serving and undemocratic, and seek to mobilize the former against the latter" (Kazin 1998: 1).

Populism as rhetoric is a double-edged sword, cutting to the right as well as the left. And that's the difficulty in relying on a "populist" spirit to produce a movement that community organizers could lead in a progressive direction. Examples abound of "populist" programs that could have been progressive but turned to the political right – from the "radio priest" Father Charles Coughlin in the 1930s to the Tea Party populists who mobilized to oppose Obama's health care program and contest the mid-term Congressional elections of 2010.

A few attempts to find common ground between left and right populists have failed on their conflicting analyses of power. Who are the anti-democratic elites? Left populists see corporate executives as an exploitative economic elite, and right populists see government bureaucrats as an unaccountable political elite. The realignment of the Democratic and Republican parties set in motion by the civil rights legislation of the 1960s and 1970s has put the two major parties on different sides of left and right populism. The Republicans welcomed the whites from the Southern, Midwestern, and Rocky Mountains states who were fleeing the Democrats' positions on racial and gender issues. By the sixth year of the Obama administration, Democrats were no longer split on foreign policy and social issues (such as abortion and birth control, gay marriage, and a path to citizenship for undocumented immigrants). Differences among the Democrats were on economic policy, between those who would deregulate Wall Street and those who would increase oversight of the financial industry. Among the Republicans the split was between the Tea Party populists who would shut down the federal government over budget negotiations and the party moderates who fear the consequences of such extreme actions (Meyerson 2013). Given these sharp contrasts, a single populist grassroots social movement uniting left and right would appear to be an elusive strategy for community organizers to pursue.

The Progressive Era

The Progressive Era in American political life is commonly understood as the period between the 1890s and the 1920s. As the historic Populist movement was dominated by issues from rural America, the Progressive movement was largely a response to the problems of urban America. It is often seen as a movement of the middle class and professionals, seeking municipal reform and scientific efficiency. The federal government established the Children's Bureau in 1912, and the Women's Bureau in 1920, the year the Nineteenth Amendment was ratified, establishing the right to vote for women. Community organizing, broadly considered, traces its roots to this period (Betten and Austin 1990). One noteworthy innovation influencing the development of community organizing was the settlement house movement, a prime example being Hull House in Chicago, founded by Jane Addams in 1889. Similar projects were established in New York, Cleveland, and other cities. This era saw the beginnings of the social work profession, and its analysis of urban problems as resulting from social disorganization, particularly among the rapidly growing communities of poor and working-class immigrants. Strategies employed in the social work tradition emphasized consensus, working with the powers that be, and the development of such institutions as community centers, community chest programs, maternal and child health clinics, public kindergartens, and other social services. Addams, like many Progressives, had a broad reform vision; she was a founder and the first president of the Women's International League for Peace and Freedom, and was awarded the Nobel Peace Prize in 1931 (Elshtain 2002).

The Progressive movement is also known for its efforts to reform the industrial system. Immigrant workers were joined by wealthy Progressives from the Women's Trade Union League to improve factory wages and working conditions. The tragedy of the Triangle Shirtwaist Factory fire in New York in March 1911, in which 146 people died – 122 young immigrant women and two dozen men – shocked New York. The disaster opened a window of opportunity for political reform. The New York state legislature established the Factory Investigating Commission, sparking the first protective legislation governing the employment of women and children, unemployment insurance, workers' compensation, minimum wages, and maximum working hours. Frances Perkins, the head of the New York Consumers League, who happened to be at Washington Square on the fateful day of the fire and observed the carnage, was appointed to the Factory Commission. When Franklin D. Roosevelt was elected President in 1932, he appointed Perkins as the first Secretary of Labor and the first woman cabinet secretary (von Drehle 2003). The Progressive alliance of poor and working people with the liberal middle class and professionals presents a model that has found new forms in contemporary community organizing practice.

The New Deal

The stock market crash of October 1929 triggered the Great Depression that lasted through most of the 1930s and led to FDR's New Deal. Urban problems were redefined as resulting from powerlessness and exploitation. The fundamental interests of poor and working people were seen by many as conflicting with the interests of economic and political elites. FDR pulled together a coalition of labor, liberals, big city political machines that mobilized working-class white ethnic groups and urban blacks in the North, and lower- and middle-income whites in the South. One of FDR's first pieces of important legislation, the National Industrial Recovery Act, was declared unconstitutional by the Supreme Court. Its vital Section 7A on labor's right to organize and bargain collectively was, however, passed in the National Labor Relations Act of 1935 (the Wagner Act). Other key legislation affecting labor included the Social Security Act of 1935 and the Fair Labor Standards Act of 1938.

The limits of the New Deal coalition were set by the Southern Democrats, who often composed a majority of the Democratic votes in the House and the Senate in the 20-year period from 1932, when FDR was first elected President, to 1952, the end of Harry Truman's Presidency, when Republican Dwight Eisenhower was elected President. The consequence of Southern Democrats dominating the New Deal Congressional majority was the elimination of any aspects of legislation that threatened white supremacy and segregation in the South. Agricultural and domestic workers, for example, were excluded from the protections of the Fair Labor Standards Act. When it became clear that organized labor might succeed with its "Operation Dixie" drives, Southern Democrats supported weakening the Wagner Act with the Labor Management Relations (Taft–Hartley) Act of 1947 (Katznelson 2013: 150–9, 161–82).

The Unemployed Councils organized by the Communist Party brought a new militancy to the urban scene in the 1930s as neighborhoods were mobilized to attempt to block evictions and to demand jobs for the unemployed (Fisher 1994: Ch. 2). Most significantly, the revived labor movement, under the leadership of John L. Lewis, president of the United Mine Workers of America (UMWA), began the campaign to organize industrial workers. In 1935 Lewis provoked a walkout from the American Federation of Labor (AFL) to form the Committee on Industrial Organization (CIO), in a highly dramatic fashion (Alinsky 1970), which we will elaborate on in the next chapter. Lewis oversaw the organization of the steel, auto, rubber, and packinghouse workers – and became Saul Alinsky's hero. Lewis's theatrical rhetoric, audacity, and militancy would have a strong impact on Alinsky's ideas about organizing, influencing him to build his very first people's organization, the Back of the Yards Neighborhood Council, in 1939, which rode the wave of the union movement in Chicago's meat-packing companies.

The Great Society

The civil rights movement provided the spark and the energy that drove the reforms of the 1960s and 1970s. The Supreme Court's

1954 decision in *Brown* v. *Board of Education*, litigated by the legal defense fund of the NAACP, was the beginning of the end of legal segregation in the American South. A mass movement began with the Montgomery Bus Boycott at the end of 1958, and produced a network of ministers in the SCLC. College students initiated the lunch-counter sit-in movement in 1961, joined the Freedom rides in 1962, and formed their own organization, SNCC. The African American civil rights movement, with its master frame of equal rights, inspired related movements among other minorities, including Hispanics, Asian Americans, and Native Americans, and eventually cascaded on to movements of women, gays and lesbians, people with disabilities, and others.

Alinsky built two essentially all-black organizations, The Woodlawn Organization (TWO) in Chicago and FIGHT in Rochester, New York. He was, however, often critical of civil rights groups for emphasizing short-term mobilization over long-term organization and for relying on charismatic leaders rather than patiently developing new local leadership. Nevertheless, as we shall see in Chapter 2, Alinsky's program was revived by the era of civil rights, and experience with that movement inspired many of the younger men and women who became organizers over the following decade.

2

Saul Alinsky and the Industrial Areas Foundation

How did Saul Alinsky become a subject of controversy in the Presidential elections of 2008 and 2012, despite having died 40 years earlier? To understand why Alinsky shaped community organizing the way he did, it helps to know something about Chicago in the first half of the twentieth century. Chicago is central to several characteristic aspects of Alinsky's approach to community organizing. The background of corrupt political machines, Alinsky's education at the University of Chicago, his early career as a criminologist, his first experience in building a people's organization during a union campaign in the Back of the Yards neighborhood – all contributed to his distinctive brand of organizing.

Chicago

Driven by a flood of European immigrants, Chicago grew from a city of a half-million people in 1880 to 2.7 million in 1920 and nearly 3.4 million by 1930. Industrial conflict was dramatically expressed in the Haymarket Riot of 1886 and the Pullman Strike of 1894. The settlement house movement and the new profession of social work attempted to aid the transition of European immigrants, many coming from a peasant background, to urban industrial America. When the First World War cut off immigration from Europe and postwar legislation greatly restricted entry, the way was clear for migration of African Americans from the South to Chicago. Blacks increased from 2 percent of Chicago's population in 1910 to 7 percent in 1930 (Bulmer 1984: 12–13; Lemann 1991: 61–107, 225–305).

Chicago rapidly developed a deserved reputation for political corruption. Infamous political machines included those of William Hale ("Big Bill") Thompson, mayor from 1915 to 1923, and again from 1927 to 1931; and Edward Joseph ("Ed") Kelly, mayor for three terms from 1933 to 1947. Kelly was allied with Patrick A. Nash, sewer contractor and chairman of the Cook County Democratic Committee (together known as the Kelly–Nash political machine). With the start of Prohibition in 1920, Chicago's gangsters, politicians, and police were caught up in a web of criminal enterprises. Violence between criminal factions approached the level of warfare, with the Al Capone gang coming out on top, for a time.

Award-winning novelist Nelson Algren, who called Chicago the "city on the make," wrote about the perennial battle between reformers and scoundrels:

> Big Bill greeted his fellow citizens correctly then with a cheery, "Fellow Hoodlums!" The best any mayor can do with the city since is just to keep it in repair. Yet the Do-Gooders still go doggedly forward, making the hustlers struggle for their gold week in and week out, year after year, once or twice a decade tossing an unholy fright into the boys. And since it's a ninth-inning town, the ball game never being over till the last man is out, it remains Jane Addams' town as well as Big Bill's. The ball game isn't over yet. But it's a rigged ball game. (Algren 1951: 19)

Rough-and-tumble Chicago presented a macho image, which Alinsky was eager to embrace in order to appear "street-wise" and conversant with gangsters, hustlers, and political bosses. He nevertheless always wore conservative attire, prompting one observer to call him a man who "dressed like an accountant and talked like a stevedore." The machismo inherent in this persona had the unfortunate effect of biasing Alinsky against women working as organizers or playing leading roles in community organizations.

Only in the 1970s would his successors begin to draw on the full potential of women for grassroots leadership.

Alinsky was born in Chicago in 1905. His father was a Russian-Jewish immigrant, and his mother, his father's second wife, was a Jewish immigrant from Belorussia. Saul shared their orthodox Jewish faith, and was religious until his early teens, when he decided he was an agnostic. His father, a tailor, was reserved and distant, while his mother was volatile and argumentative, a troublemaker. Saul took after his mother. His parents divorced when Saul was 13, and his father moved to California. During the school year, Saul lived with his mother in Chicago; summers he would spend with his father in California, which became a kind of second home to him.

The University of Chicago

By the end of high school, Alinsky had become a good student. He majored in archeology as an undergraduate at the University of Chicago, then switched to sociology to work on a Master's degree when the Depression appeared to eliminate any prospects for him finding work as an archeologist (Horwitt 1989: 3–9). The sociology department at the University was the first in the United States, and the only one for some time with a coherent collective focus – empirical studies of the rapidly growing metropolis of Chicago. Emphasizing field research, case studies, and social surveys, the Chicago School of Sociology, as it became known, had distinctive methodological approaches that ranged from participant observation to social mapping to statistical analysis of demographic information (Bulmer 1984). Under the leadership of Robert E. Park and Ernest W. Burgess the department faculty and graduate students published studies of such urban phenomena as hobos, gangs, ghettoes, dance halls, and the like. For Park and Burgess, deviance and criminality were not the result of heredity, but rather were the product of the disorganization of ghetto life.

The Chicago sociologists took pains to distinguish their discipline from the field of social work. Alinsky would do the same, often speaking dismissively of social workers and other "do-gooders" – provoking an animosity toward him among some social work faculty that continues to the present day. Alinsky drew on Chicago School research methods when approaching new communities. He would instruct his organizers to begin work in a community by doing an institutional and power analysis, typically involving numerous personal interviews of leaders in the neighborhoods they had been invited to help organize.

The University of Chicago was also home to the philosopher John Dewey, whose pragmatism had a strong influence beyond the philosophy department. Pragmatism resonated well with the practical sensibility of the sociology department's case method. Dewey's pragmatist colleague George Herbert Mead had considerable influence on the sociology department as well as the emerging field of social psychology (Rucker 1969: 13, 132–57). This pragmatic spirit would keep Alinsky focused on the practical and immune to the ideological appeals of the leftists he often worked with in the 1930s and 1940s.

Alinsky entered the University of Chicago in the fall of 1926. When he began his junior year by enrolling in Ernest Burgess's course in social pathology, he was assigned to a field project as a participant observer in a Chicago public dance hall, collecting personal life histories by interviewing patrons. He enjoyed working at the edges of conventional society and adopting the pose of the tough, savvy guy who knew his way around. In the spring 1929 term he took Burgess's course on organized crime, and became fascinated with the connection between delinquent youth and social disorganization.

Alinsky began work with Burgess's graduate assistant Clifford Shaw at the Institute for Juvenile Research (IJR) on a study of delinquent boys in a teenage Italian gang on the near West Side. Before he could complete work on a Ph.D. degree, however, Alinsky dropped out of the University and went to work for the Illinois Division of the State Criminologist at the Illinois State Penitentiary at Joliet, where he spent most of his time for the three years from 1933 to 1936. Although he did well, he found work with the hardened adult prisoners at Joliet less satisfying than working with the youth gangs. Nevertheless, his experiences

23

there gave him a fund of great stories that he never tired of telling (Horwitt 1989: 10–33).

John L. Lewis and the CIO

The National Industrial Recovery Act (NIRA) of 1933 was one of President Franklin Roosevelt's major responses to the Great Depression that contributed to his winning the Presidential election in 1932. Section 7A of the NIRA gave workers the right to organize "unions of their own choosing" and bargain collectively with employers. Although, as we saw in the previous chapter, the Supreme Court declared the framework of the NIRA unconstitutional, the Section 7A provisions were written into the National Labor Relations Act ("Wagner Act") of 1935. The AFL, composed largely of craft unions, was reluctant to devote significant resources to organize industrial unions. However, John L. Lewis, president of the UMWA, took advantage of the new legislation to organize virtually all of the bituminous coal industry under a uniform contract. At its peak, the UMWA had some 800,000 coal miners in its ranks.

When the AFL met for its 1935 convention in Atlantic City, New Jersey, Lewis was prepared to lead the CIO out of the AFL and operate independently, bankrolled by the newly filled treasury of the UMWA. Lewis provoked an argument on the convention floor with William Hutcheson, president of the Carpenters' Union. Their altercation ended with Lewis punching Hutcheson in the face and leading the CIO unions out of the convention. Two years later the CIO had 3.4 million members in 32 national unions with over 500 locals. Lewis's bold organizing campaigns, eloquent rhetoric, and skill at bluffing made a strong impression on Alinsky, as we noted in the previous chapter.

Back of the Yards

By the end of 1936, Alinsky had left Joliet prison and was back in Chicago working at the IJR for Clifford Shaw in his Chicago Area

Project. Shaw sent Alinsky to the Back of the Yards neighborhood to combat juvenile delinquency by developing a neighborhood association, controlled by local people, that could provide youth at risk with recreation, counseling to stay in school, and help in finding jobs.

Meanwhile the Packinghouse Workers Organizing Committee (PWOC) was attempting to organize the industry. The meat-packing industry was dominated by four large companies – Swift, Armour, Wilson, and Cudahy – that were determined to defeat the union drive. Eight smaller meat-packing companies were known as the independents.

Working conditions in the stockyards and meat-packing plants were not very far advanced beyond those described by Upton Sinclair in his 1909 muckraking novel, *The Jungle*. But organizing was not easy. Workers were divided by skill, ethnicity, and race. Three elements among the packinghouse workers were strong supporters of the union: the veterans of an unsuccessful strike in 1921 (many of these now worked for the independents), black workers won over by the "culture of unity" promoted by the union, and finally the Communist Party (CP) organizers (Halpern 1997: 96–112; Horowitz 1997: 58–83). Alinsky was very impressed by the PWOC's organizers. He watched them recruit members, conduct mass meetings, develop issues, and raise money – all skills of professional radicals (Finks 1984: 13–18), many of which he made part of his organizer training. Alinsky no doubt enjoyed John L. Lewis's response when asked if he was worried about his employment of Communists in CIO organizing drives: "Who gets the bird, the hunter or the dog?"

But the PWOC ran into a tough problem – opposition from the Catholic Church. The majority of Back of the Yard residents were Catholics. The largest nationality group were Poles, but there were also Lithuanians, Slovaks, Bohemians, Germans, and Irish as well as Mexicans. Rivalries and animosities ran high among the ethnic groups, each with their distinct parishes, grammar schools, religious societies, and athletic clubs. Many Catholic officials opposed the PWOC because of the involvement of the CP. The PWOC's lead organizer for Chicago was a charismatic young CP member,

Herb March. Women associated with the PWOC, led by CP member Vicki Starr, developed projects for youth, and attempted to draw Alinsky to support their efforts (Horwitt 1989: 56–76; Lynd and Lynd 1973: 67–87). (Vicki Starr would be reintroduced to the New Left as "Stella Nowicki" in the 1974 documentary film *Union Maids*. No longer a member of the CP, Starr used the alias because she was still organizing – a clerical union at the University of Michigan – at that time.)

While working for Clifford Shaw's IJR, Alinsky had met Joseph Meegan, a high school teacher and part-time park recreation director. They made plans to organize a neighborhood council that would deal with all the pressing issues of the community, not just youth concerns. Meegan and his wife were well-connected Catholics, and his brother was a priest serving as an aide to Bishop Bernard J. Sheil, Chicago's senior auxiliary bishop and key assistant to Cardinal George W. Mundelein.

During the spring and summer of 1939, Alinsky and Meegan worked to bring together every group they could talk into participating in the new organization. On July 14, 1939, the Back of the Yards Neighborhood Council (BYNC) held its constitutional convention, with over 350 delegates representing 109 organizations (Finks 1984: 17). They approved a constitution, determined priorities for the next year, and voted support for the PWOC, and elected Herb March as a director of the Council. The BYNC adopted as its motto: "We the people will work out our own destiny" (Horwitt 1989: 147). Two nights later the BYNC took part in a major CIO rally at the Chicago Coliseum. With Alinsky's encouragement, Bishop Sheil shared the stage with John L. Lewis, effectively giving the Catholic Church's blessing to the CIO organizing drive. In the weeks following the rally the major packinghouse companies agreed to recognize the union (Finks 1984: 17–18; Horwitt 1989: 71–6).

Clifford Shaw fired Alinsky, angry that his own objective of a youth council in Back of the Yards had been abandoned in favor of the latter's more ambitious plan. Neighborhood pressure forced Shaw to backtrack, but Alinsky began to look for support that would give him independence to follow his success with the BYNC in additional neighborhoods in Chicago and other cities (Finks 1984: 19–26). Alinsky's contractual association with the BYNC ended in the 1950s. The organization grew increasingly conservative, and resisted efforts of African Americans to move into the area, prompting Alinsky to comment that he might have to form another organization to oppose the BYNC. Nevertheless, Meegan remained the lead organizer of the BYNC for many years, a counter to the position preferred by Alinsky of rotating organizers from "outside" a community after a brief term, usually two or three years.

Although Alinsky frequently disparaged academics during his career, Donald and Dietrich Reitzes (1982) argue that his sociology studies at the University of Chicago, combined with his experience in Joliet, the CIO organizing drives, and his work in Back of the Yards, gave him a coherent theory of power, organization, and community that shaped his approach to community organizing. The Chicago School's rejection of individual, psychological explanations of crime led Alinsky to focus on the community. The promise of political power serves to unite the often-fragmented elements within a low-income community as a single organization. This then forms a stable instrument with which to bargain with the establishment that exercises control over the decisions affecting a community. The use of conflict tactics serves to bind a community together in a common identity around its common interests, which contrast with the interests of its opponents. Such tactics as picketing, boycotts, and strikes can push an adversary to compromise and negotiate a settlement. The Chicago School focus on interviewing individuals outside the mainstream led Alinsky to emphasize the training of effective community leaders as an important force fostering citizen engagement in political affairs. Promoting grassroots leadership remains a central priority of community organizing today.

The Industrial Areas Foundation

In early 1940, Alinsky received invitations to bring his organizing skills to two additional packinghouse cities: Kansas City and South St. Paul. Neither project went very well. Alinsky was short of money and organizers. Bishop Sheil had introduced Alinsky to Chicago financier Marshall Field III, who encouraged Alinsky to incorporate the IAF to serve as the nonprofit vehicle for his organizing work. Field became chairman of the IAF board of trustees, who committed to raise $15,000 a year for five years to support Alinsky to develop projects in additional industrial cities. Besides Field and Bishop Sheil, the IAF board included Stuyvesant Peabody (executive of the Peabody Coal Company), Judge Theodore Rosen of Philadelphia, Britten Budd (a utilities manager), G. Howland Shaw of the US State Department, and Kathryn Lewis, daughter of John L. Lewis (Finks 1984: 23–4).

When the United States entered the Second World War in 1941, IAF trustee Shaw got Alinsky a job promoting war bonds and serving as a roving ambassador to defense industry plants, making use of his close ties to CIO leaders. Alinsky also used the war years to work on his first book, *Reveille for Radicals*, describing his ideas and experiences. During this time he became friends with the French Catholic philosopher Jacques Maritain, who was in exile in the United States during the war. Maritain encouraged Alinsky to finish his book, and became an advocate for him among the Catholic hierarchy. A decade later in 1958, Maritain arranged a meeting for Alinsky in Milan with Archbishop Giovanni Montini (later named Pope Paul VI). For three afternoons Montini and Alinsky discussed the possibility of the IAF organizing among workers there as it had in Back of the Yards, building a working-class organization as an alternative to the Italian Communist Party, which was growing increasingly popular among Italian workers. Montini arranged for Alinsky to have an audience in Rome with Pope Pius XII. But the Vatican did nothing to implement Alinsky's proposal, and an IAF project in Italy never got started (Finks 1984: 114–19).

Reveille for Radicals

Reveille for Radicals was a surprising best-seller when it was published in 1946 by the University of Chicago Press, and made

Alinsky known to a national audience. The first part of the book, three chapters under the heading "Call Me Rebel," is a rhetorical celebration of the American radical as the wellspring of democracy, in the tradition of Thomas Paine (a quote from Paine serves as an epigraph for the book). The second and longer part of the book, eight chapters under the heading "The Building of People's Organizations," is constructed around an idealized version of Alinsky's experience in Back of the Yards. *Reveille* claims that the BYNC model was spreading successfully, although in reality Alinsky had only struggling projects in Kansas City and South St. Paul. The book emphasizes developing local leadership, the inevitability of conflict as a people's organization becomes powerful, and the special role of the organizer. In the important new Introduction and Afterword to the republished 1969 Vintage edition (see Alinsky 1989), Alinsky brought his ideas up to date, as we shall see toward the end of this chapter.

California and the Community Service Organization

Alinsky had been working since 1945 to put together a sponsoring committee to finance an organizing project in California. One evening he was playing cards with friends from the University of Chicago when sociologist Louis Wirth complained about Fred Ross, an employee of the American Council on Race Relations, which Wirth directed, in California. It seems that instead of doing community research, Ross was organizing Mexican Americans. Alinsky perked up and concluded he needed to meet this guy.

On a trip to Los Angeles in 1947, Alinsky met with Ross and was immediately impressed, offering him a job with one of his floundering projects in the Midwest. Ross persuaded Alinsky to let him try to organize Mexican Americans in California. Alinsky raised money from a group of progressive Jewish businessmen in Los Angeles, and Ross was hired by the IAF at a salary of $3,000 a year. Ross, who had been organizing Unity Leagues among Latinos in the Boyle Heights area of Los Angeles, met with the young activists associated with Edward Roybal, who had just made an unsuccessful run for the Los Angeles City Council.

Planning to continue to campaign for public office, Roybal had formed the Community Political Organization to keep his supporters together. Alinsky told Ross the group would have to change its name to the Community Service Organization (CSO) if it hoped to receive funds from the IAF. The group agreed to the name change, and Ross went to work. He told Alinsky that the Mexican American communities in California lacked the infrastructure of churches, clubs, and associations that Alinsky had used in Chicago to build an organization of organizations. Ross convinced Alinsky to let him try to build an individual membership organization using house meetings to bring together families and neighbors to discuss how they might tackle community issues. Ross helped build a CSO membership of 1,000, who then conducted a registration drive that signed up 15,000 new voters, tripling the voting strength of Mexican Americans in Los Angeles (Burt 2007: 53–96; Finks 1984: 41).

Just as Alinsky's fortunes were looking up, he was stunned by the death of his wife Helene in a swimming accident in the summer of 1947. His responsibility for their two children helped him work through his despondency. The next year he threw himself into writing an "unauthorized" biography of John L. Lewis (Alinsky 1970). Alinsky admired and possibly imitated a number of characteristics of Lewis's style: "the aggressiveness, the gamesmanship, the deliberately provocative challenges and insults to opponents, first the promotion of conflict, then the negotiated resolution of it to win political advantage; the use of power" (Horwitt 1989: 219).

The CSO in Los Angeles had become a great success. Backed by a coalition of Latinos, labor (especially the Steel Workers and the Garment Workers), Jewish progressives, and the left, Roybal won his race for City Council in 1949, becoming the first Mexican American councilman in 70 years (Burt 2007: 79–94). He won his bid for reelection to the Council in 1951 by an even larger margin, and went on to serve 13 years on the Council, followed by 30 years in the US House of Representatives. But in 1950 Alinsky told Ross the IAF was running out of money, and he would have to raise his own support. In 1952 Ross took a job in the San Francisco Bay Area. He proceeded to organize the first CSO chapter outside the Los Angeles area in San José. One of the first people to turn up was a young man named Cesar Chavez.

Although he had failed to obtain grants from the Ford and Rockefeller Foundations, Alinsky's fundraising efforts finally achieved substantial results in 1953 with a three-year grant of $150,000 from the foundation of the late liquor businessman Emil Schwarzhaupt. Alinsky promptly rehired Ross as the IAF West Coast director, and Ross convinced Alinsky to hire Cesar Chavez as a field organizer to help expand the CSO. Over the next dozen years the Schwarzhaupt Foundation's executive secretary, Carl Tjerandsen, a former University of Chicago graduate student, would award over $3 million to support the IAF and its associated projects (Bardacke 2011: 69–70).

The IAF Builds a Successful Individual Member Organization

Ross and Chavez traveled up and down the Central Valley organizing new CSO chapters. Other organizers were soon added to the CSO staff, including Dolores Huerta and Gilbert Padilla, who would become co-founders with Chavez of the National Farm Workers Association in 1962. Roybal had been selected as the first president of the CSO, but resigned after his election to the Los Angeles City Council in 1949. Los Angeles steel worker Tony Rios was elected the next president, and was to win a path-breaking victory over the Los Angeles Police Department in a 1952 brutality case in which he was beaten by two police officers (Burt 2007: 117–33).

Frank Bardacke summarizes the impact of the CSO as follows: "By 1962 [the CSO] would have over 10,000 members in thirty-two chapters from Sacramento to Calexico that had registered 400,000 new voters. . . . Far more than any other organization, the CSO was responsible for the more than one hundred Mexican

American politicians who won California local elections in the 1950s and early '60s" (Bardacke 2011: 87). Ironically, an individual membership organization (rather than an organization of institutional members) became one of the most successful early Alinsky projects. But aside from claiming the association with Cesar Chavez, the IAF today seldom mentions the CSO, as it does not reflect the IAF's exclusive reliance on institutionally based organizations – and primarily congregation-based ones at that. Nor does the IAF make much mention of Fred Ross, although it continues to use the house-meeting techniques Ross pioneered.

Chavez became executive director of the CSO in 1960, but resigned from the organization two years later when he failed to persuade the CSO convention to support his proposal to shift emphasis to organizing farm workers. Huerta, Padilla, and Ross later followed. The CSO began to decline by the mid-1960s, hurt by the loss of its exceptional organizing staff, and overshadowed by Chavez's UFW and militant new groups like the Mexican American Political Association (MAPA).

Other key organizers joining the IAF staff in this period included Nicholas von Hoffman, who worked for Alinsky for 10 years, from 1953 to 1963, and went on to a career in journalism; former Admiral corporation executive Tom Gaudette in Chicago, who later worked as an independent organizer and consultant through his Mid-American Center; and Catholic seminarian Ed Chambers, who would become Alinsky's successor at the IAF.

The Woodlawn Organization

As we noted in Chapter 1, despite his frequent criticism of civil rights leaders and social movements that emphasized mobilization over organizing, Alinsky found that the civil rights movement sparked new opportunities for his work in the 1960s. Catholic leaders in Chicago had asked Alinsky to help organize the black community on the south side of the city.

Work to form TWO had proceeded slowly under the direction of the IAF's lead organizer, Nicholas von Hoffman. One day in 1961, however, a former TWO volunteer telephoned von Hoffman from a New Orleans hospital, at the end of a Freedom Ride on a Greyhound bus that had met with violence from the Ku Klux Klan. The former volunteer asked von Hoffman to work with the Chicago chapter of the Congress of Racial Equality (CORE) to co-sponsor a meeting in which participants in the Freedom Ride from Chicago would report on their experience. Von Hoffman was skeptical, later writing, "up to that time, a civil rights meeting in the community could be held in a claw-foot bathtub" (von Hoffman 2010: 184). To his astonishment, however, several hundred people turned out to hear the Freedom Riders, crowding the church where the meeting was held, and spilling out into the street. Over $600 was raised for CORE by passing the hat (Finks 1984: 134–6). Von Hoffman telephoned Alinsky in California and told him, "we should toss out everything we are doing organizationally, and work on the premise that this is the moment of the whirlwind . . . we are no longer organizing but guiding a social movement." Alinsky immediately perceived the winds had shifted, and returned to Chicago the next day (Horwitt 1989: 399–401).

Woodlawn became the first black community organized by Alinsky. The IAF's work with TWO was supported by grants from Catholic Charities of Chicago, the Schwartzhaupt Foundation, and the Presbyterian Church – adding an important dimension of Protestant financing. The area had already been battered by a proposal known as the Hyde Park–Kenwood urban renewal plan. Some 20,000 people, mostly poor blacks and whites, would be displaced, and housing for middle- and upper middle-income people developed. There were no provisions in the plan for the people who would be forced to move. Although von Hoffman and Fr. Jack Egan had opposed the plan, it was approved in 1958.

TWO's anticipated battle would be with the University of Chicago, which wanted to develop a South Campus by demolishing a mile-long strip of land in the community. But first, following the successful CORE rally for the Freedom Riders, TWO initiated a voter registration drive. Charges in the legislature of vote fraud in Cook County had led to a purge of the voter rolls, requiring all eligible voters to register again. TWO decided to demonstrate its clout by chartering 46 buses to carry over 2,000 Woodlawn area residents to City Hall to register. The success of this "Northern Freedom Ride" got the attention of city officials, strengthened the standing of TWO, and sparked further growth for the organization (Horwitt 1989: 401–5).

TWO held its first convention in March 1962, with 1,200 delegates representing some 90 community groups, including 13 churches. Alinsky arranged for Mayor Richard J. Daley to give the welcoming speech, and Rev. Ralph Abernathy of the SCLC to give the keynote address. Rev. Arthur M. Blazier, pastor of the local Apostolic Church of God, was elected president (Horwitt 1989: 414–20; Silberman 1964: 319). After a tough two years of bargaining, TWO won the right to negotiate on behalf of the Woodlawn community with the University of Chicago.

Alinsky's work received widespread publicity when Charles Silberman, a writer for *Fortune* magazine, concluded his 1964 book on contemporary race relations, *Crisis in Black and White*, with a chapter on TWO titled "The Revolt Against 'Welfare Colonialism.'" Silberman criticized the welfare and settlement house approach as perpetuating dependency and demoralization. "TWO's greatest contribution," he wrote, "is its most subtle: it gives Woodlawn residents a sense of dignity." Silberman gave a strong endorsement of Alinsky's approach: "TWO is the most important and the most impressive experiment affecting Negroes anywhere in the United States" (Silberman 1964: 318, 348).

By the end of the 1960s, after Alinsky ended the IAF's formal relationship with TWO, the group began to run government-funded service programs such as job training and innovative schools. When this funding ended, TWO moved toward community economic development, and dropped its early emphasis on mobilizing citizen participation (Warren 2001: 46).

The War on Poverty

In the wake of President John F. Kennedy's assassination in 1963, and pushed by the ascendant civil rights movement, President

Lyndon Johnson maneuvered a remarkable series of reform legislation through Congress: including the Civil Rights Act of 1964,
the Voting Rights Act of 1965, and the Economic Opportunity Act
of 1964, which established the Office of Economic Opportunity
(OEO) to direct his "War on Poverty." Alinsky's ideas had at
least a modest foothold in War on Poverty, particularly through
Richard Boone, another graduate of the University of Chicago's
sociology department and a criminologist, who was working for
Senator Robert Kennedy's Committee on Juvenile Delinquency
in 1963. As part of the task force putting together the legislative
package for the OEO, Boone pushed to include the requirement
that the new community action agencies have the "maximum
feasible participation" of the poor – a phrase that received little
notice as the Economic Opportunity Act was passed, but soon
became one of the most controversial provisions of the anti-
poverty program (Horwitt 1989: 475–7; Lemann 1991: 149–53).
Daniel Patrick Moynihan (1969) later described it as a "maximum
feasible misunderstanding." Alinsky denounced the entire War
on Poverty as "political pornography," and ridiculed the idea
that federal funds could be used to empower the poor. However,
his reservations hadn't kept him from serving as a paid consultant to an OEO contract with the University of Syracuse to train
community action organizers. Alinsky brought in Fred Ross from
California to run the one-year training program, but it proved
controversial, and the contract was not renewed (Horwitt 1989:
478–82).

Unhappy with the controversies over community action programs generated between the OEO and mayors in cities across
the country, Congresswoman Edith Green of Oregon got language attached to an appropriations bill in 1967. Her "Green
Amendment" provided that mayors would have the power to
appoint one-third of the board members of community action
agencies – usually enough to control the organizations. Only
rarely would poor people genuinely have the opportunity to
run a community action program, however briefly, as was the
case with CDGM, the multi-county Head Start program of
the Child Development Group of Mississippi (Dittmer 1995:

363–88; Greenberg 1990). The political controversy created by Mississippi's two segregationist Senators ensured that CDGM's federal funding would not last for long. Community organizing would have to return to its tradition of seeking funds from its members and other private sources.

FIGHT

Rochester, New York, provides another example of Alinsky riding the waves of the civil rights movement and responding to the growing black revolt in northern cities. Rioting in its inner city ghettoes in the hot summer of 1964 shocked the city officials of Rochester. Concerned members of congregations were reading Silberman's *Crisis in Black and White*, and soon had organized an ecumenical group of ministers to invite Alinsky and the IAF to come and help them organize. Alinsky shifted organizer Ed Chambers from TWO in Chicago to Rochester, and he assisted a council of ministers to develop a black-controlled organization to be called FIGHT (for Freedom, Integration, God, Honor, Today). After only two months of organizing, some 2,000 people attended its founding convention in June 1965. Minister Franklin Florence was elected president, and FIGHT adopted a program prioritizing equal employment opportunity. White allies would be steered into a separate organization, Friends of FIGHT.

By the fall of 1966, FIGHT was ready to begin negotiations with Rochester's major employers. Xerox Corporation quickly agreed to a small experimental program that would determine what training approaches would work to qualify black employees for permanent positions. This rapid success prompted FIGHT leaders to set their sights on Rochester's largest employer, Eastman Kodak, with 41,000 jobs in the city. Kodak proved to be a much tougher case. After months of negotiations, a senior executive signed an employment training agreement with FIGHT in mid-December. Within hours the new chief executive of Kodak and its board of directors had repudiated the agreement, an action FIGHT called the "Christmas massacre."

Alinsky and FIGHT organized a shareholder battle with Kodak, soliciting churches that held Kodak stock for proxies to vote at Kodak's annual meeting in April 1967. FIGHT threatened to organize a national pilgrimage to Rochester by its supporters, and Stokely Carmichael promised to organize a national boycott of Kodak products. Daniel Patrick Moynihan entered the conflict as a mediator between the two antagonists, and after a few weeks of secret negotiations announced an agreement that resolved the issues dividing them.

With the IAF having completed its three-year commitment, Alinsky withdrew from Rochester in the spring of 1968. At FIGHT's fifth convention in the following year, an insurgent faction ousted Minister Florence. Within two years the leader of this revolt had left Rochester, and the organization disbanded in the early 1970s.

Alinsky in the Late 1960s and Early 1970s

Methodical training of community organizers by the IAF dates from 1969, when Midas Muffler founder Gordon Sherman gave Alinsky a $200,000 grant, matched by another $200,000 for trainee scholarships from the Rockefeller Foundation (Finks 1984: 233–4). Alinsky finally had the funding he needed to begin training a significant number of organizers and leaders. The money came just as he was beginning to savor the national recognition he had received as a result of his work with TWO and FIGHT, and the chapter on the IAF in Silberman's *Crisis in Black and White*.

Weary after years of difficult work with little money and staff, Alinsky found he enjoyed invitations to speak on college and university campuses across the country. He admired the energy and concern of students active in civil rights and the New Left, although he judged their efforts misdirected. Efforts to set up meetings between Alinsky and the SNCC and Students for a Democratic Society (SDS) often ended in frustration as Alinsky usually managed to alienate the young activists.

Reveille *Reprint and* Rules for Radicals: *Alinsky Has the Last Word*

The 1969 reprint of *Reveille for Radicals* (see Alinsky 1989), with its significant new Introduction and Afterword, and the publication of the long-delayed *Rules for Radicals* (1972) gave Alinsky an opportunity to revisit, revise, and clarify a number of his earlier ideas. According to the "Afterword" he wrote for the reprinted edition of *Reveille* in 1969, he was planning to call the new book *Rules for Revolution*. Someone – whether Alinsky or his editor, we don't know – thought better of that. "Revolution" was a word taken up by a number of groups in the "new communist movement" in the late 1960s and 1970s (Elbaum 2002), and could have misrepresented Alinsky's intentions. The final title thus substituted "Radicals."

Alinsky had come to realize that his "three years and out" rule – that his organizers ought to spend no more than three years in a community before a local organizer should be able to take over – was not working well. He accepted that a long-term relationship with organizations founded with help from the IAF would be needed (Horwitt 1989: 530).

Alinsky's approach to community organizing has been criticized for being bound to the scale of neighborhoods, and thus unable to have an impact on the most important issues facing poor communities. Yet Alinsky was well aware of the need to affect policy on a wider scale, although he was unable during his lifetime to marshal the money and the trained organizers to implement that strategy. In the "Afterword" to the 1969 reprint of *Reveille*, he wrote:

> A political idiot knows that most major issues are national, and in some cases international, in scope. They cannot be coped with on the local community level. The Back of the Yards Council at the zenith of its power could not deal with its most pressing problem of its time, the issue of widespread unemployment, until our whole economy boomed as a result of world developments. (Alinsky 1989: 225)

From a strategic perspective, Alinsky saw that he would have to put together numerous "people power organizations" all across the country, and that finding the organizers to make that happen would be a challenge:

> ... in order to create a national movement one must first build the parts to put together. The building of the parts is a tough, tedious, time-consuming, often monotonous and frequently frustrating job. There is no detour to avoid this means to the end of building a national movement. (Alinsky 1989: 226)

Alinsky's interaction with the young leaders of the New Left and the civil rights movement during the 1960s did not give him much encouragement about the prospects for recruiting these energetic young people:

> The fundamental issue is how we go about building a national move-ment when so many of the present generation do not want to undergo the experience in time or detail of the organization of its parts, or of the local areas of organization. . . . Either they do not want to do the tough and tedious job of building the parts, or are incapable of it, or it is a combination of both. (Alinsky 1989: 226)

Alinsky had come to see that organizing the poor alone would not be enough; they would need middle-class allies in order to build a majority movement:

> Our poor are in the minority so that even if we organize all the blacks, Mexican-Americans, Puerto Ricans, and Appalachian whites and create a coalition, they will still need allies for the necessary power for change. These allies can only come from organized sectors of the middle class. (Alinsky 1989: 234–5; see also Alinsky 1972: 184–5)

In these statements toward the end of his career, Alinsky summed up his strategic vision for change. His goals are national in scope, and require skilled and dedicated organizers who can build powerful organizations with trained and mentored grass-roots leaders who can construct a cross-race and cross-class coalition – a program reminiscent of the Popular Front of the

1930s. Alinsky did not anticipate that there would be at least three networks vying for national leadership with little inclination to cooperate with each other, and that his own IAF would be the most reluctant to lead nationally. In this strategic vision he was, and remains, ahead of the majority of his followers today.

But Alinsky had little opportunity to promote the ideas in his long-awaited *Rules for Radicals*, or to guide the IAF into a new era training organizers. He died suddenly and unexpectedly in 1972 from a heart attack on the streets of Carmel, California, at age 63. Always the rebel, Alinsky left this final challenge: "This is the job for today's radical – to fan the embers of hopelessness into a flame to fight" (Alinsky 1972: 194). Ed Chambers would be relatively free to institutionalize Alinsky's tradition as he saw fit.

The IAF after Alinsky

When Saul Alinsky died in 1972, Ed Chambers was training director for the IAF. As Alinsky's designated successor in the event of his death, Chambers took over responsibility for the IAF program. The organization looked to be a dead duck. There were only two organizers – Chambers and Dick Harmon – and a secretary left on the staff. Chambers' challenge was to figure out how to do what Alinsky had never quite managed: to train enough organizers to build a network of community organizations capable of taking on metropolitan and regional issues, and eventually be able to impact state and national policy on issues of concern to poor and disenfranchised people. The IAF had to judge what had been idiosyncratic to Alinsky and his times, adapt to changes in society since the 1930s and 1940s, and respond to the backlash against the social movements of the 1960s and 1970s. Training would have to be systematic and consistent in order to spread a common approach to organizing that could be replicated on a large scale.

The Modern IAF

The IAF sees its organizational history divided into two periods: the "early IAF," when Alinsky was director, from 1940 to 1972, and the "modern IAF," directed by Chambers from 1972 to 2009 and continuing to date. Chambers introduced four significant changes to Alinsky's organizing model: first, an emphasis on congregation-based organizing; second, a regional structure (gradually consolidated to Metro IAF in the East and Midwest, and West/Southwest IAF); third, placing relational organizing and leadership training at the center of its work; and, finally, professionalizing the training and compensation of organizers (Industrial Areas Foundation 1999: 106) – as resource mobilization theory had predicted "the professionalization of reform."

The IAF refers to its organizing activity as "broad-based" rather than "congregation-based," but this is something of a misnomer (see Hart 2001: 255). By "broad-based," the IAF means that it includes a variety of religious congregations – Protestant, Catholic, Jewish, and occasionally Muslim; represents major ethnic communities – African American, Latino, and white; and takes in affluent suburban congregations in addition to poorer inner city ones. The result should be the alliance between the poor and the middle class that Alinsky had foreseen as necessary for success in building power. To the IAF, "broad-based" means that they will no longer build all-white groups like Back of the Yards Neighborhood Council or all-black groups like TWO and FIGHT; it will emphasize building racially integrated groups. On the other hand, the "early IAF" under Alinsky developed organizations with a broad base in a wider sense – including unions, civic groups, neighborhood associations, and advocacy organizations in addition to religious congregations.

There are several additional features of the modern IAF. A typical IAF organization, Chambers writes, is composed of "some political conservatives, lots of moderates, and some liberals" (Chambers 2004: 15). Whatever happened to those "radicals"

Alinsky spoke of in *Reveille for Radicals* and *Rules for Radicals?* San Francisco-based organizer Mike Miller quipped that a book on the contemporary IAF should be titled "Reveille for Moderates" (Miller 1992). Although Chambers nevertheless titled his book *Roots for Radicals*, he began by defining "radical" down: "'Radical,'" he wrote, "is from a Latin word that means 'root.' Radical means going to the roots of the matter, and the roots of the spirit. A radical is a person who searches for meaning and affirms community" (Chambers 2004: 13).

At first Alinsky did not anticipate a long-term involvement with the organizations he would help start. He imagined his organizers would spend three to five years with a group and then leave it to its own developed leadership and to a locally recruited organizer who would replace the IAF's professional. The tension between short-term and long-term involvement would shift. "This did not work out," he was forced to admit (Horwitt 1989: 530).

The modern IAF would have to address two primary problems: recruiting, training, and retaining organizers, and identifying, training, and developing leaders. As Alinsky had noted, "Since organizations are created, in large part, by the organizer, we must find out what creates the organizer. This has been the major problem of my years of organizational experience: the finding of potential organizers and their training" (Alinsky 1972: 63). Alinsky enumerated some of the qualities he saw as making the ideal organizer: curiosity, irreverence, imagination, sense of humor, a blurred vision of a better world (as opposed to a sharp, ideologically defined vision), an organized personality, strong ego, open mind with political relativity, and the ability to create the new out of the old (Alinsky 1972: 72–80). Chambers instituted better job stability for the IAF organizers by eliminating the "three-year rule." Community organizing now could be a career, with skilled staff retained by offering a ladder of advancement, enough money to support a family, the stability of a longer stay in a community, and another job opening when it was time to move.

A Theology of Organizing: Healing the Body Politic

As a one-time seminarian, Chambers retained an interest in theology, and gave thought to connecting organizing with religious teachings. On one level this meant using biblical references and stories to support points about organizing. But getting at a deeper substantive point, in 1978 under Chambers' direction, the IAF released a pamphlet, "Organizing for Family and Congregation," to set a direction for the IAF training program and explain the reasons why its organizers would work to build congregation-based organizations. (Many of these key early documents have been compiled in Schutz and Miller 2014.)

It began by discussing the "war over values" in terms that borrowed both from the populist right's critique of American liberal culture (the "culture wars" of the 1970s and 1980s) and the populist left's critique of market society and capitalism. "Intermediate voluntary institutions" – churches, civic clubs, and the like – were weak, and the middle was collapsing, leaving no effective force to counter the influence of "huge corporations, mass media, and 'benevolent' government." The theory of "mediating structures" had been popularized in a 1977 booklet by sociologist Peter L. Berger and Richard John Neuhaus (1996); they pointed out that their "mediating structures" were compatible with the Catholic Church's doctrine of "subsidiarity." Institutions of greed and unaccountable power were displacing families and churches. Families were feeling a "decreasing sense of integration, centeredness and confidence" (Chambers 1978: 3–4). Fewer Americans participated in traditional civic clubs, voluntary associations, and fraternal groups (Skocpol 2003). Individuals were increasingly alienated and isolated; "bowling alone," as Robert Putnam (2000) would put it. Congregation-based organizations, the IAF argued, could become the mediating institutions that strengthen families and congregations. Relational organizing was thus a response to the culture of isolation, *de facto* racial and socio-economic segregation, and individualism that had transformed American society.

Chambers (1978: 18) explained his vision of the citizens' organization built around the religious congregation: "Religious institutions form the center of the organization. They have the people, the values, and the money. Without church people, moderates and conservatives as well as liberals, citizens' groups can get sucked into movements or relationships which can actually weaken family life or church life" (Chambers 1978: 18).

Starting from Alinsky's critical comments on the social movements of the 1960s, Chambers defined the approach of IAF organizers and leaders in contrast to activists in movements. The weaknesses of movements, as the IAF saw it, were "a lack of collective leadership, the reliance on charismatic leaders, the lack of a solid dues base, the tendency toward unaccountable action, and the alienation of moderates and conservatives" (Chambers 1978: 5). In contrast to movement ideologies that would appeal only to a radical remnant, the IAF's moderate organizations would "speak for the whole."

From Alinsky's zest for conflict and confrontation, Chambers shifted the IAF to a style emphasizing negotiation and compromise – which could be seen as a move from populism to pluralism. For Chambers, as with Cortes in Texas, relationships established through one-on-ones, house meetings, and other elements of relational organizing amount to developing the social capital of the community. Dennis Shirley, in his study of the IAF's "alliance schools" educational projects in Texas, makes a useful distinction among "*finance capital,* which designates the value of money; *human capital,* which refers to an individual's intellectual and physical capabilities; and *social capital,* which comprises the values embedded in social relationships" (Shirley 2002: xiv).

In part, Chambers' move toward religious congregations resulted from the relatively greater decline in labor unions, civic associations, and fraternal orders in the 1950s and 1960s. The campaign to drive the Communists out of the labor unions caused many unions to withdraw from alliances with progressive groups. Although some of Chambers' exhortations sound as if they were meant as "timeless truths," in fact they are a response to a particular time and place, just as Alinsky's early programs were a response to his times.

The IAF in Texas

Some of the IAF's most successful projects have been based in Texas, where Communities Organized for Public Service (COPS), founded in San Antonio in 1974, became the model for IAF state director Ernesto Cortes, Jr. In the process of building a powerful network of affiliates, collectively known as Texas Interfaith, Cortes reinforced Chambers' inclination to reorient the IAF toward working mostly with religious congregations. Texas also became the first example of how several CBCO affiliates within a state could work together to impact policy on the state level.

Cortes was not breaking new ground organizing among Mexican Americans in San Antonio, although he certainly introduced a productive new approach. Texas had given birth to two of the first Hispanic civil rights organizations, the League of United Latin American Citizens (LULAC), founded in 1929 (Marquez 1993), and the American GI Forum, founded by Dr. Hector Garcia after the Second World War in 1948 (Allsup 1982). In the wake of John F. Kennedy's Presidential campaign in 1960, the GI Forum and LULAC had come together to form an explicitly political organization, the Political Association of Spanish-Speaking Organizations, which in 1963 engineered the first defeat of the Anglo elite in south Texas, in Crystal City. In 1966 UFW organizer Gilbert Padilla led a wildcat melon strike at La Casita Farms in Starr County. Despite some success, the strike collapsed and the UFW retreated to focus on California. The short-lived La Raza Unida party had a brief period of success in the early 1970s, electing officials in Crystal City before falling apart in conflict (Shirley 2002: 1–7). William C. ("Willie") Velasquez, one of the founders of the Mexican American Youth Organization in the late 1960s, started the Southwest Voter Registration Education Project in San Antonio in 1974 (Gómez-Quiñones 1990: 128, 166).

Ernesto Cortes entered Texas A&M University in 1959, the first in his family to attend college. He graduated three years later with a double major in English and economics. He started graduate work in economics at the University of Texas, but dropped out to get involved with social activism. He worked with the UFW, heading up the statewide boycott of La Casita melons from Starr County as well as the grape and lettuce boycotts. While working on the boycotts he met Padilla, who told him about Alinsky's work with Fred Ross and Cesar Chavez building the CSO in California. After the collapse of the melon boycott, Cortes went to work with the Mexican American Unity Council to develop minority-run businesses in San Antonio.

In 1971 Cortes had an opportunity to visit Chicago and talk with IAF training director Ed Chambers. He returned with a group from San Antonio in 1972 for a 10-day training, and stayed on to work with IAF projects in Chicago, Milwaukee, and Lake County, Indiana. Cortes returned to San Antonio in 1973 and began working to put together COPS.

It proved to be a propitious moment for developing a people's organization in San Antonio. The Good Government League, created by the Chamber of Commerce in 1954 to select and elect candidates to the city council, had been dominated by a core group of old Anglo families. Their control of the city council was being challenged by a group of builders and developers who wanted rapid growth (Rogers 1990: 75–8, 101). This latter group developed a slate of independents who succeeded in winning seats on the council, and even elected an independent mayor in 1973. As the political process model of social movements would predict, this split in the ranks of the elite created a window of opportunity for political influence by an insurgent organization from the Hispanic community.

Cortes soon found that his base of support was strongest among the Catholic parishes serving the Mexican American community in San Antonio. Hispanic priests were eager to have the church take on the problems of poverty and discrimination experienced by their parishioners. Many priests became important leaders in COPS. Cortes also recruited many women from the parish councils and committees. COPS was supported by San Antonio's

Archbishop Furey and Patricio Flores, the first Mexican American bishop in the United States. COPS received funding from the archdiocese as well as from the local Catholic parishes, and received its first grants from the Catholic Campaign for Human Development, a national program founded in 1970 to support community organizing.

In 1977 San Antonio had its at-large system of electing the city council overturned by a federal court under the Voting Rights Act. COPS supported amending the city's charter by holding a referendum to shift to a district system, which passed. In the first election under the new district system, 5 of the 10 council seats were won by Hispanics and one by an African American. The domination of the city by the old Anglo elite was broken. Henry Cisneros won the at-large mayoral race in 1981, becoming the first Hispanic mayor of the city in 140 years (Rogers 1990: 119; Warren 2001: 53). COPS played an important role in the election by interviewing candidates and educating its members on the candidates' positions on COPS budget priorities (Boyte 1984: 146).

In its early years COPS was able to win substantial improvements in infrastructure for the poorly served Mexican American neighborhoods in San Antonio – sewerage and drainage systems, health clinics, libraries, and a community college on the south side of town. This was the time when significant federal funding was available for poor and disadvantaged communities through the Great Society programs launched by President Lyndon Johnson. COPS focused its efforts on the Community Development Block Grant (CDBG) program, as it was active in most of the neighborhoods that qualified for CDBG funds. COPS found it could negotiate its fair share of bond packages that helped fund these civic improvements. One of COPS' greatest successes was obtaining funding to rehabilitate some two thousand homes and build another thousand new affordable houses. In its first 20 years of work, COPS estimated in 1994, it had helped win nearly $1 billion worth of neighborhood improvements from various sources. COPS did not administer any of this funding itself, refusing to accept any government support (Warren 2001: 47–57).

Once COPS was thriving, it became a model for developing

similar organizations in other major Texas cities. Cortes had left San Antonio for Los Angeles in 1976 to develop the United Neighborhoods Organization in the Mexican American community in east Los Angeles for the IAF. Chambers sent organizer Arnie Graf to San Antonio to continue the IAF's relationship with COPS for the long term. In Houston a group of Protestant ministers and Catholic clergy began work on The Metropolitan Organization (TMO), and in 1978 Sister Christine Stevens, chair of the TMO sponsoring committee, persuaded Cortes to come back to lead the expansion of the IAF in Texas. Facing down some opposition from conservative Catholics, TMO held its founding convention in 1979. Other affiliates developed include Allied Communities of Tarrant (ACT) in Fort Worth and surrounding Tarrant County, and the El Paso Inter-religious Sponsoring Organization in El Paso – which faced even greater opposition from conservative Catholics – Austin Interfaith, Dallas Interfaith, and Border Interfaith in the Rio Grande Valley. Having moved its direction from reliance on the Mexican American community and Catholic parishes with COPS in San Antonio to the "broad-based" organizations exemplified by ACT in Fort Worth and TMO in Houston, the IAF rethought San Antonio and moved to organize the Metropolitan Congregational Alliance to include middle-class congregations in the suburbs.

Alliance Schools

The development of a dozen affiliates in the major cities across Texas opened the possibility of the IAF influencing policy on the state level for the first time. In the early 1980s the IAF was ready to take on the dismal state of education in Texas. A position paper, "The IAF Vision for Public Schools: Communities of Learners," was drawn up. The IAF's standing in policy-making was greatly enhanced when Democrats swept the statewide offices in the election of 1982, led by Governor Mark White and five-term Lieutenant Governor William P. Hobby, Jr. White named billionaire Ross Perot to chair a commission to come up with recommendations. The commission advocated no classes of more than 22 students, increased pay for teachers, and two years of pre-kindergarten for poor children. The education reform bill and a $4.8 billion revenue package were pushed through the Democratic legislature (Collins 2012: 75–8; Warren 2001: 72–85).

The decline in oil prices in the early and mid-1980s led to an economic recession in Texas, which contributed to White's defeat in his bid for a second term in the election of 1986. It is also believed that White's unpopular "no pass, no play" policy, which prohibited student athletes from varsity sports (especially football) if they failed any classes, doomed his candidacy. The IAF faced a more difficult time under Republican governor Bill Clements in his second (non-consecutive) term. But with the election of Ann Richards as governor in 1990, the IAF again had a friend in the statehouse. Richards brought in Lionel "Skip" Meno from New York to serve as Commissioner of Schools, and named former COPS chair Sonia Hernandez as Director of Education Policy in the governor's office. The IAF convinced Meno to try working with its organizers to engage parents and community members in improving the schools in poor districts. In 1990 the Rockefeller Foundation, with Henry Cisneros newly added to its board, agreed to fund the experiment, and the Alliance Schools program was launched. From an initial program of 21 schools in 1992, the effort soon expanded to include some 100 schools by 1996. Working with education consultants, the IAF drew up a position paper, "The Texas IAF Vision for Public Schools: A Community of Learners." The IAF argued for a shift from "students as passive learners to that of a community whose members are committed to learning the skills of problem solving, teaching themselves and collaboration" (Warren 2001: 81–5).

In 1994 Richards was defeated in her bid for reelection by George W. Bush, beginning a long period of Republican ascendancy. Since 1994 no Democrat has been elected to statewide office in Texas. The IAF is fond of saying it does not engage in partisan politics (which is true in the narrow sense that it does not endorse candidates for office), and that it has "no permanent friends, and no permanent enemies." Nevertheless, it is clear that Texas Interfaith's objectives have been more readily achieved under

Democrats than Republicans. Despite continuing activity by Texas Interfaith's affiliates, big victories are scarce, and neither the IAF nor its leaders or member groups get a mention in a recent popular survey of Texas politics (Collins 2012).

Organizing Congregations

In his study of IAF projects in Texas, political scientist Mark Warren made some shrewd observations about the differences among the ethnic and denominational types of member congregations. He identified the distinctions in congregational involvement and ministerial participation in four types of congregations: Hispanic Catholic parishes, Black Protestant churches, White Protestant denominations, and Jewish congregations (Warren 2001: 191–210). Although his observations were based on the IAF in Texas, the distinctions have a considerable degree of generality for congregation-based community organizing across the United States.

Catholic parishes have the advantage of a long history of Catholic social thought, beginning with the 1891 Papal encyclical *Rerum Novarum* by Leo XIII. Vatican II meetings (1962–5) further stimulated thinking on the church's role in obtaining economic justice. The institutional hierarchy of the Catholic Church has continued to support the role of the church in defending the poor, despite a growing conservatism in theology and social thought. Support from the parish priest, who, unlike many Protestant ministers, can't be fired or transferred by his laity, is an important element in a congregation's participation in the IAF. Some Hispanic priests, however, have had to be persuaded to pursue their social justice concerns in the political arena.

African American Protestant congregations have a rich theological tradition with themes of freedom and deliverance from oppression. Black ministers played a crucial role in the civil rights movement and many continue to work for social justice and are already involved in political campaigns. Some black pastors have been challenged to shift from a focus on racial justice to the multiracial alliances and community building in the IAF approach. In contrast to Catholic priests, black pastors are accountable to their congregations, and have to be careful not to get too far in front of them.

The Anglo congregations in the IAF are primarily drawn from the mainline Protestant churches. They tend to be less neighborhood-centered, often drawing members dispersed over a wider suburban area. White ministers participating in the IAF tend to share a background in the social gospel.

Jewish congregations have a rich theological tradition with themes of liberation and justice. They share some of the difficulties of the mainline Protestant denominations of congregations that have moved from the central city to the suburbs, and this can present problems in participation of members who fail to see their self-interest reflected in the issues addressed by the IAF affiliate.

The IAF in the Northeast

Other pioneering groups in the post-Alinsky era include organizations developed in New York, Baltimore, and Philadelphia. Queens Citizens Organization, founded in 1976, and East Brooklyn Congregations (EBC), founded in 1978, along with the South Bronx affiliate, became important forces in New York City (Industrial Areas Foundation 1990). EBC, under the leadership of Rev. Johnny Ray Youngblood of the Community Baptist Church, set up Nehemiah Homes (the reference is to the biblical leader who rebuilt the wall of Jerusalem) to build 2,100 low-cost houses and became a model for federal housing assistance. IAF lead organizer Michael Gecan described its achievement:

> An organization with a core budget of three hundred thousand dollars a year, a staff of four, and a modest headquarters in a local apartment complex halted two decades of burning, deterioration, and abandonment by building a critical mass of owner-occupied town houses and generating a chain reaction of other neighborhood improvements. EBC built on every large parcel and abandoned block in the area – 140 vacant acres. The market value of the housing built now exceeds $400 million. (Gecan 2002: 13)

In the process, the EBC faced off with New York mayors from Ed Koch (1978–89) to David Dinkins (1990–3) and Rudy Giuliani (1994–2001). Given the hard-ball big-city politics of the Northeast, the IAF remained more confrontational here than in Texas or the West. Gecan describes the kind of relationship the New York organizations worked to develop: "We wanted a more public relationship, where there was mutual respect, mutual understanding, some agreement, some disagreement, and the right amounts of tension and formality, engagement and distance. . . . an intricate and long-term public relationship – the periods of cooperation and the period of confrontation and mutual antagonism" (Gecan 2002: 109, 125).

In 1979 Chambers dispatched Gecan to Baltimore, where BUILD (Baltimoreans United in Leadership Development) was having trouble. Gecan spent 15 months reorganizing a dysfunctional organization by bringing in new congregations and developing new leaders. When Gecan moved to New York to work with the EBC, Arnie Graf took over the lead organizer position with BUILD, which found its footing and went on to develop innovative afterschool programs and its own portion of Nehemiah Homes.

In 1994 BUILD developed the country's first living wage campaign, focused on such minimum wage jobs as janitors, bus drivers, and private security guards. It succeeded in getting a law passed that increased the minimum wage to be paid by companies with service contracts with the city from $6.10 an hour in 1996 to $7.70 an hour in 1999 (Gecan 2002: 78; Pollin and Luce 2000). BUILD's success sparked a national movement that passed living wage laws in 41 cities by 2000, and 125 cities and counties by 2012 (Luce 2012). As the IAF had not placed a priority on developing shared national programs, it was not in a position to lead the living wage movement it had launched. Instead the national living wage campaign was led by ACORN, as we will discuss in Chapter 5. The newer networks would be quick to push their advantage with successful programs to multi-state and national levels.

The IAF has stayed focused on metropolitan and state policies and programs, and has been reluctant to develop a national agenda, despite having much of the base Alinsky hoped to achieve in order to influence the issues that could only be addressed at the national level. Insofar as the IAF had a national program, it was led by the affiliates in the Northeast, from Boston through Washington, DC, under the leadership of Gecan and Graf (Swarts 2010). Recently an umbrella organization, Metro IAF, was formed by 22 affiliates in the Northeast, Southeast, and Midwest, apparently to develop the capacity to work on national issues. On its website, Metro IAF claims credit for all the accomplishments of its affiliates going back at least as far as 1990. The IAF conducts National Training programs of seven days during the summer, and Regional Leadership Trainings of five days. As of 2013, the IAF had 59 affiliates in 21 states, Canada, the United Kingdom, Australia, and Germany.

The IAF on the Move

By the late 1970s the two most celebrated IAF-launched projects in Chicago, the BYNC and TWO, were no longer affiliated with the IAF. Tom Gaudette's neighborhood organizations in Chicago were independent and not affiliated with the IAF. Chicago's Cardinal Cody withheld funding from the IAF, ending the Archdiocese's support that had sustained Alinsky's organization since the 1930s (Warren 2001: 47). The IAF had projects underway in New York, Baltimore, Texas, and Los Angeles (Northcott 1985: 18). Chambers moved the IAF headquarters to New York in 1979, stating that the IAF had to give closer attention to its projects in the Northeast and Mid-Atlantic states (Chambers 2004: 114).

The move from Chicago to New York made sense for the IAF, helping it focus on innovative programs in the Northeast and in Texas. But it left the Midwest relatively open to new organizing efforts, and greatly increased the IAF's distance from California. This proved to be an opening that PICO National Network exploited on the West Coast, and the Gamaliel Foundation found to its advantage in the Midwest. Both groups built up a regional presence from the mid-1980s to the mid-1990s. At the same time, the Direct Action and Research Training Center (DART) became established in Florida. It looked for a moment as if these four community organizing groups would be regional networks, dividing the country among themselves. But this was not to be. As the number of local community organizations grew rapidly over the decade from 1985 to 1995, the IAF, PICO, and Gamaliel each aspired to become a national network, as we will discuss further in Chapter 5. They began to compete with each other for influence, money, power, and affiliates.

Chambers writes that beginning in 1991, Mon. Jack Egan began enticing the IAF to return to Chicago. Chambers finally brought the IAF office back to Chicago in 1994. He retired in 2009, but the IAF – unlike PICO National Network and the Gamaliel Foundation, which chose new directors from their ranks and moved on – was not prepared to select a successor. Instead, a quadrumvirate consisting of four senior IAF organizers – Cortes, Stephens, Gecan, and Graf – rotated administrative responsibilities among themselves for one-year terms. Like bishops, the old guard held on to their regional turf. The IAF sees its leadership in a kind of apostolic succession in the history of organizing: from John L. Lewis, to Saul Alinsky, to Ed Chambers (Industrial Areas Foundation 1999: 9). Apparently the continuing line of succession is not clear. In any event, as of early 2014 no puff of white smoke has issued yet from the IAF Vatican in Chicago. Instead the IAF for administrative purposes has divided itself into two organizations: "West/Southwest IAF," led by Cortes and Stephens, and "Metro IAF" in the East and Midwest, led by Gecan and Graf.

Further innovation would come from newer networks of community organizations, as we will examine in Chapter 5, after first exploring the organizing worldview in Chapter 3 and additional components of the organizer's toolbox in Chapter 4.

3

An Organizing Worldview

A specific set of concepts shape the perspective or worldview that guides community organizers in the Alinsky tradition as they work for social change. The mix includes such perspectives as the nature of power and its sources; the distinction between "the world as it is" and "the world as it should be"; the balance between self-interest and values; leadership development; the distinction between organizers and leaders; and the importance of public relationships. Above all, the Alinsky tradition emphasizes that it is necessary to develop multi-issue organizations in order to build power. A distinctive definition is given to many of the key terms; understanding just what these words mean is a central purpose of the training conducted by the networks. None of these elements are unique to the Alinsky tradition; but their inclusion in a complex pattern of activity constitutes a distinctive organizing subculture. Absorbing this subculture reshapes the identities of organizers and leaders especially.

Organization

Community organizers build carefully structured organizations with engaged, active members. Alinsky was clear that it is essential to build multi-issue organizations: "A single issue is a fatal strait jacket that will stifle the life of an organization. . . . Many issues mean many members" (Alinsky 1972: 120).

What is so special about organizations? Organizations develop leaders, carry out campaigns, hone and refine long-range strategies, sustain and expand political relationships, mobilize members and allies, test tactics to see what works in which circumstances, win victories, consolidate gains, defend advances against backlashes and counter-movements, evaluate actions, sum up experiences, pass on lessons learned, and keep people together through the doldrums so they can resume the advance during the next window of political opportunity.

A. Philip Randolph, the leader of the Brotherhood of Sleeping Car Porters from 1925 to 1968, and one of the most important early leaders of the African American civil rights movement, put it this way: "At the banquet table of life, there are no reserved seats. You get what you can take and keep what you can hold. If you can't take anything, you won't get anything. And if you can't hold anything, you won't keep anything. And you can't take anything without organization" (from a plaque in Union Station, Washington, DC).

Organization in Successful Social Movements

Over the last hundred years, four great social movements in the United States – the African American freedom movement, the labor movement, the women's movement, and the conservation/ environmental movement – used sustained organization-building as a crucial means for their battles for structural changes to expand American democracy. An example – the Montgomery Bus Boycott, which triggered the civil rights movement of the 1950s and 1960s – illustrates the power of organized people to overcome seemingly overwhelming odds.

Case Study: The Montgomery Bus Boycott
Today in almost every American elementary school, children learn the story of Rosa Parks, a tired seamstress in Montgomery, Alabama, returning home after work on December 1, 1955, who refused to move from her seat on the bus even when faced with arrest, and thus started the civil rights movement that overthrew legal segregation in the American South.

Pete Seeger wrote a song about her, with the line "When Rosa Parks sat down, the whole world stood up." Simple, no? In another context, Seeger commented, "A good song is sometimes a triumph of oversimplification." Yes, indeed.

We now know the reality was very different from the elementary school morality tale (see Dreier 2006; Loeb 2004). As she made clear in her autobiography, Rosa Parks was a dedicated long-term activist for civil rights. Her husband, Raymond Parks, had worked to defend the Scottsboro Boys in the 1930s. She joined the Montgomery branch of the NAACP in 1943 and served as its secretary. She registered to vote in 1945, and was inspired by the NAACP's branch director, Ella Baker, who traveled through the South in the early 1940s. Parks also worked closely with E.D. Nixon while he served as president of the Montgomery NAACP branch and during his term as president of the Alabama state NAACP. Nixon was also the Alabama representative of the Brotherhood of Sleeping Car Porters, reporting to the union's president, A. Philip Randolph. In addition, Parks assisted Nixon in his Brotherhood responsibilities (Parks 1992; see also Brinkley 2000).

Montgomery had another notable organization in the Women's Political Council, led at that time by Jo Ann Gibson Robinson on the faculty of the historically black Alabama State College. Nixon called Robinson when Parks was arrested on the bus that Friday afternoon, and Robinson stayed up all night mimeographing flyers calling for a bus boycott on Monday morning, December 4. Council members distributed them throughout the black sections of Montgomery on Saturday afternoon and evening. As Nixon prepared to leave Montgomery on Saturday for a shift as a Pullman porter, he met with a sympathetic reporter for the Montgomery newspaper, which ran a front-page story on the planned boycott in its Sunday edition.

Another experience that contributed to Rosa Park's decision to be arrested was her participation in a 10-day workshop at the Highlander Folk School in Tennessee, headed by Myles Horton. Parks learned of the workshop from Virginia Durr, an important white ally, and the wife of Clifford Durr, an attorney who returned to Montgomery after working as a New Deal administrator and member of the Federal Communications Commission (Durr 1985). The Durrs were well connected in Washington, DC; Virginia's sister was married to former Alabama Senator and then

Supreme Court Justice Hugo Black. At the Highlander workshop, people from throughout the South shared stories of their work to oppose the segregation system.

These groups of activists in Montgomery managed to organize over the weekend a nearly total boycott of the buses that Monday by a black community of some 40,000 people – truly a remarkable accomplishment, and one made possible only by the prior relationships of trust and commitment made through organizing. On Monday night a mass meeting was held and the Montgomery Improvement Association was formed to continue the boycott. A new pastor, Rev. Martin Luther King, Jr., was elected as its chairman.

Not only did the black community have the strong ties of the local church congregations, the NAACP branch, and the Women's Political Council, they also had "weak ties" to Washington, DC (through the Durrs), and to the labor movement (through E.D. Nixon to A. Philip Randolph, and through Randolph to Walter Reuther of the United Auto Workers) in New York and Detroit, as well as the network of Highlander contacts throughout the country. Contacts with national NAACP officials also meant access to the resources of the NAACP Legal Defense Fund, which litigated matters relating to the boycott. It was the "strength of weak ties" (see Gladwell 2000: 53–5) that would be most valuable in raising money to support the year-long boycott, providing legal services, and publicizing the event in national media, thus helping to make Martin Luther King, Jr. a national spokesman for civil rights.

Against Organization

Let's give a brief hearing to the leading contrarians on the subject of organization and making change. The classic argument against organization as a vehicle for social change is Robert Michels' *Political Parties* (1959), first published in English translation in 1915. In Michels' view, "the iron law of oligarchy" holds that even democratic socialist parties like the Social Democratic Party of Germany will become oligarchical as leaders gain specialized knowledge of politics not available to their mass membership and their goals become deflected toward their self-interest of personal job security. A variation of Michels' thesis was argued by Frances Fox Piven and Richard Cloward in their book *Poor People's Movements* (1979). Despite inequality and exploitation, the authors note, the lower classes seldom mobilize to demand change. Only under exceptional circumstances of structural crises in economic and social institutions can the poor mobilize and win changes that support their interests. Institutional changes are mediated by the political system, and reforms are possible only in conditions of serious electoral instability.

Piven and Cloward argue that economic and political elites are drawn together over time to form one ruling class. Political institutions act as the instruments of economic elites. Only in times of social upheaval do segments of the ruling class develop different interests and divide among themselves. In the interest of retaining their elective offices, some politicians may offer the lower classes reforms that economic elites oppose. Segments of the economic elites soon learn to live with the reforms and even turn them to their advantage. Piven and Cloward argue that the demands raised by the formal organizations of the poor count for little; political elites completely determine the response. Organizers and leaders of people's organizations typically act to blunt the disruption of mobilized protest, and are eventually co-opted. Finally, the requirements of maintaining mass-membership organizations lead to those conservative tendencies that Michels termed "the iron law of oligarchy." Piven and Cloward conclude from this gloomy analysis that the only productive strategy is to escalate disruptive protest by "pushing turbulence to its outer limits" (Piven and Cloward 1979: 91). The best way to accomplish this is not a formal, mass-membership organization, but through a network of cadre groups able to coordinate mass mobilizations and confrontations.

In support of their thesis, Piven and Cloward present four case studies, two from the 1930s and two from the 1960s. They make their best case that few lasting reforms were made by the formal organizations of the unemployed in the 1930s and welfare recipients in the 1960s. Their historical presentations of the industrial union movement in the 1930s and the civil rights movement of the 1950s and 1960s, however, undercut their argument. Unions were able to force corporations to concede resources that could sustain their organizations over time. The civil rights movement was able to draw in middle-class support and build organizations that could in quiescent times consolidate, defend, and even expand gains made in times of turmoil. In the end, Piven and Cloward's critique of organization – part-anarchist and part-Michels-ist – and their oversimplified view of the state as a tool of economic elites are dramatic but unconvincing (see Walls 1980).

Power

As community organizers work to build powerful organizations, getting local leaders – especially clergy – past the negative connotations of power is obviously important. Power is defined as the "ability to act effectively in the world" (M. Miller 2012: 3). "Power over" is distinguished from "power with." The point is easier to grasp with the Spanish word *poder*, a verb for "to be able to," which is also the noun "power." A well-known example is the use of the phrase "Si, se puede!" by Cesar Chavez, "Yes we can!" – a memorable phrase borrowed by Obama in his 2008 Presidential campaign, and an empowering reversal of a discouraging old saying, "No se puede," "It can't be done."

Many people immediately think of Lord Acton's epigram, "Power tends to corrupt, and absolute power corrupts absolutely." But this is "power over." "Power with" can be benign if the people who wield and exercise power are kept accountable by their constituency. Dennis Jacobsen, a Lutheran pastor and director of Gamaliel's National Clergy Caucus, observes that "powerlessness also corrupts" (Jacobsen 2001: 39).

An organization's power is not developed to be used in a symbolic sense. The goal of organizing is not to "speak truth to power," but to gain power. PICO's principles of power are that "Power respects power," "Power is taken, not given," and "Power defines the rules" (Block 2012d: 118–19). Alinsky, meanwhile, argued that "Power is not only what you have but what the enemy thinks you have," and "Power has always derived from two main sources, money and people" (Alinsky 1972: 126–8).

Going further: advocacy is not what community organizations say they do. Broad-based community organizations are vehicles through which oppressed, marginalized, and exploited people speak powerfully for themselves directly through mass action and through leaders they elect. Community organizations have elaborate training programs and activities that identify current and potential leaders and develop their capacity for effective civic action. As North Bay Organizing Project organizer Davin Cardenas says, "Dolphins need advocacy; poor people need power." Nor does community organizing engage in "expressive" actions or "gesture politics," where there is little if any prospect of winning.

Power is a complex phenomenon. Political scientist Steven Lukes (2005) argues that there are "three faces of power" we must account for. The first, one-dimensional, familiar view of power concerns the making of decisions on issues over which there is a clearly understood conflict of interests. This is the usual kind of power a community organization wants to exercise to win on an issue. The second dimension of power concerns the ability to remove an issue from the arena of public discussion, through the mobilization of bias, creating a "non-decision," which never receives general public attention. The third dimension of power concerns the deeper absence of a sense of alternatives to the status quo, resulting from myths, ideologies, or the suppression of information. The dominant elements of society have created the values, beliefs, and legitimations that result in certain ideas being either inconceivable or not taken seriously. This third dimension of power is similar to what the Italian activist and theorist Antonio Gramsci termed "hegemony." Challenging power at this level would require a strategy of transformative change that so far has been beyond the scope of community organizations (see Hart 2001: 62–5). Analyzing the power structure of any given community, particularly the opposition to the issue a group hopes to win, is one of the tools of the trade covered in Chapter 4 below under "power analysis."

"*The World As It Is*" vs. "*The World As It Should Be*"

The outlook on "the world as it is" has been influenced by the tradition of Christian realism, typified by the work of Reinhold Niebuhr, and his realistic view of human nature. The good human society does not emerge spontaneously; it requires serious citizen engagement to assure a decent measure of social justice. It also requires acknowledging the importance of self-interest in human motivation and behavior (Hart 2001: 51–2).

One of the remarkable continuities in the week-long training programs of the IAF, PICO, and Gamaliel national networks is reading and role playing the section on "The Melian Dialogue" from Book Five of Thucydides' *History of the Peloponnesian War* – a favorite text of Alinsky's (see Horwitt 1989: 531; Thucydides 1954). Typically this exercise comes early in the program, on the first or second day. The discussion raises the question of whether the inhabitants of the island of Melos, a colony from Sparta that had refused to join the Athenian empire, should accept the offer from Athens to become its colony. The Melians would pay tribute to Athens, but would be free to enjoy their own lives and property. The Athenians noted that they had the power to enforce this arrangement, and urged the Melians to adopt a realistic assessment of the "world as it is"– as opposed to the "world as it should be" (the Melians wish to remain neutral and be no one's colony). If they refuse the Athenian offer, the Melians will be defeated, with their military-age men slaughtered and their women and children sold into slavery by the Athenians. The Athenians warn the Melians that it is foolish to expect Sparta to intervene to defend them from Athens. But the Melians rely on hope and idealism. Eventually they are defeated by Athens, the men are killed, and the women and children sold into slavery as threatened.

The discussion turns to "modern Melians" – which the IAF sees as typical of activists in the peace, anti-nuclear, and environmental movements, for example – self-righteous, given to wishful thinking, full of principled rhetoric, reducing conflicts to either/or choices, unwilling to bargain or compromise. Stephen Hart writes, "The moral of the story, in training, is that organizing deals with real life and death issues, and that witnessing to high ethical values and relying on moral persuasion are at best inadequate, often useless, and sometimes harmful" (Hart 2001: 52).

A favorite scriptural reference is Matthew 10:16, where Jesus says to his disciples, "I send you out as sheep among wolves, be therefore wise as serpents and innocent as doves." Or in everyday terms, be tender-hearted but tough-minded. Even Marxists have their version, with Antonio Gramsci's masthead motto for *L'Ordine Nuovo*, the newspaper he edited: "pessimism of the mind, optimism of the will."

German social scientist Max Weber's famous lecture "Politics as a Vocation," given in 1918 at Munich University, drew a contrast between an "ethic of ultimate ends" (the world as it should be) and an "ethic of responsibility" (the world as it is):

> Politics is a strong and slow boring of hard boards. It takes both passion and perspective. . . . Man would not have attained the possible unless time and time again he had reached out for the impossible. But to do that, a man must be a leader, and not only a leader but a hero as well, in a very sober sense of the word. And even those who are neither leaders or heroes must arm themselves with that steadfastness of heart which can brave even the crumbling of all hopes. . . . Only he has the calling for politics who is sure that he shall not crumble when the world from his point of view is too stupid or too base for what he wants to offer. Only he who in the face of all this can say "In spite of all!" has the calling for politics. (Weber 1946: 128)

Gordon Whitman of PICO says a corollary of "the world as it is" perspective is that "you begin with people where they are, not where you want them to be" (Whitman 2006–7: 53). Ed Chambers of the IAF concludes, "To be moral is to struggle in the arena of the world as it is while guided by the values of the world as it should be" (Chambers 2004: 43).

Self-Interest and Values

The Alinsky tradition of organizing sees self-interest as a key to human motivation, and getting clear about one's own self-interest (and being able to express it clearly to others) is an important focus of training. Self-interest is something one attempts to clarify in one-on-one relational meetings. Trainers are careful to distinguish self-interest from selfishness, on the one hand, and selflessness, on the other. *Selfishness* is a "what's in it for me?" spirit that is not conducive to working with others on an issue that would benefit the community as a whole. *Selflessness*, with its "whatever you want" spirit, is a weak motivation for public action. *Self-interest*, as Aaron Schutz and Marie Sandy write, "include[s] all of those aspects of people that motivate them to act" (Schutz and Sandy 2011: 194).

As organizer Michael Jacoby Brown explains, "Self-interest includes our whole selves, our stories and memories and the relationships we have with close friends and family. It involves all that makes us tick and why" (Brown 2006: 200). Stephen Hart writes, "Self-interest does not mean looking out for number one in disregard of others, but is rather an empowering clarity and focus on one's needs, values, and purposes. . . . Or more generally, one's self-interest is really one's agenda, whether economic, social, or spiritual" (Hart 2001: 66).

This is not to say that values don't play an important part. Manuel Pastor and colleagues write:

> Community organizing has seen a dramatic shift in recent years. To slightly overstate the case, the traditional Alinsky-model of organizing was based on bringing together uncommon partners based on very narrowly-defined shared interests. Newer transformative organizing suggests that more uncommon alliances will stick if instead they are based on shared values and an expanded sense of common interest. (Pastor et al. 2013: 29)

PICO National Network has placed a special emphasis on values, asserting that organizing should be "value-driven." Jose Carrasco of San José State University, a collaborator with PICO's leadership, sees self-interest and values not as opposites but as "two different ways of looking at who one is, what one cares about, and what kind of community one is embedded in" (Hart 2001: 78).

Organizers and Leaders

A crucial focus of building broad-based organizations is the development of leaders. Schutz and Sandy state straightforwardly: "The central job of organizers is to develop leaders" (Schutz and Sandy 2011: 205). A popular definition of a leader is "one who mobilizes others toward a goal shared by leader and followers" (Wills 1994a: 66). Leaders, in other words, have followers they are able to turn out for actions. In his widely distributed essay "Finding and Making Leaders," organizer Nicholas von Hoffman wrote, "Leaders are found by organizing, and leaders are developed through organization" (von Hoffman n.d.: 1).

What makes a great organizer? Alinsky said he looked for curiosity, irreverence, imagination, a sense of humor, an organized personality, a blurred vision of the better world, and, finally, "a well-integrated political schizoid" – able to polarize a conflict one day, and bring the sides together in negotiation the next (Alinsky 1972: 72–80).

The distinction between organizers and leaders remains an essential element in the Alinsky tradition. Von Hoffman expresses one end of the spectrum on the role of the organizer in his handout paper "Finding and Making Leaders":

> . . . the good organizer should never – or virtually never – make a public speech, never get his name in the paper, never enjoy any formal authority in the organization. . . . The good organizer is the self-effacing mentor who judges his work a success when he can leave the organization without even being missed. (von Hoffman n.d.: 10)

By contrast, Eric Mann, director of the Labor/Community Strategy Center in Los Angeles, blurs the distinction between organizers and leaders. His "12 roles of the successful organizer" – foot soldier, evangelist, recruiter, group builder, strategist, tactician, communicator, political educator, agitator, fundraiser, comrade/ confidante, and cadre (Mann 2011) – include many functions that leaders within an organization could master.

The IAF formulated the "iron rule of organizing": never do for people what they can do for themselves. Easier said than followed, the rule is unclear how one determines what people are capable of doing for themselves. Mark Warren describes the tension he saw while studying the IAF:

> The IAF describes its primary task to be the development of leadership. It seeks to teach the skills, knowledge, and abilities necessary to conduct what it calls the "arts of politics." Technical skills are included here. But the emphasis here is more on teaching participants to weigh alternatives, negotiate differences, analyze power dynamics, and strategize. (Warren 2001: 212)

Seasoned organizers have a mental list of the qualities they look for when sizing up a prospective leader. For Gregory Pierce they include stability, accountability, anger and humor, patience, vision, and an understanding of power. Organizers use one-on-one meetings to develop a relationship with people who have promising potential for leadership. A person identified as a potential leader needs to be propositioned to accept a leadership role within the organization. Based on relationship and reciprocity, the offer/ challenge should be considered by the person and negotiated to meet the self-interests of both leader and organization (Pierce 1984: 88–92).

No one leader can provide everything needed to build a powerful organization. Leadership is collective, organized in core teams for each institutional member of a broad-based organization. In a pioneering study of African American women in the civil rights movement, Belinda Robnett distinguished "bridge" leadership from the formal leadership of organizations, especially at the grassroots level (Robnett 1997: 19–35). The informal leadership of women was particularly important as a complement to the charismatic leadership of the traditionally male ministers – which remains a factor in congregation-based community organizing as well. Whereas formal leaders have institutional, organizational power, bridge leaders – predominantly women – have an informal but vital power that connects the organization to grassroots members and potential members, often on a one-to-one basis.

Even the nature of charisma in leaders can differ greatly, as Gary Wills shows in his contrasting sketches of civil rights movement leaders Martin Luther King, Jr. and Robert ("Bob") Moses (Wills 1994b: 211–26). Despite all the effort to make the differences clear, there remains disagreement and tension among the roles of "activist vs. leader vs. organizer." The further you travel from the Alinsky tradition, the more blurred the distinctions become.

A related issue is the distribution of power and authority within a community organization between paid organizer staff and the volunteer leadership of the organization: officers, member organizations' representatives on the leadership council, task force chairs, and so on. Given the time the organizers have to hold one-on-ones and build relationships with leadership within the organization as well as with public officials and other influential figures in the community, it is not surprising that they end up with considerable power, presenting a tension with the idea of a democratically run organization. Warren introduces the idea of "consensual democracy" to describe the process by which agreement is reached within IAF organizations (and by extension the other CBCOs in the Alinsky tradition) (Warren 2001: 226–38). Institutional processes – "discussion, negotiation, compromise" – work to develop a consensus that also draws on the relationships among members, so that most decisions don't have to be made by majority voting among adversarial positions.

Training

Training plays a vital role in socializing new leaders to the worldview or outlook of community organizing. Some of the learning concerns basic tools and skills: doing one-on-ones, running good meetings, public speaking, handling media, scheduling time.

More complex tasks include cutting issues from problems, power analysis, negotiating, strategic planning, and fundraising.

As political scientist Stephen Hart writes, training in the conceptual language and perspectives of community organizing networks is vital to altering the worldview of the participant regarding social change:

> We might say that the terminology encodes the conclusions. That is, learning to express the concepts in the ways suggested by those who are strongly committed to organizing means accepting a good part of the perspective they advocate. . . . the focus on language is a powerful way to form participants' ideas. (Hart 2001: 80)

Local half-day trainings are just introductions – typically to the concept of power and to the skill of doing one-on-ones. Emerging leaders are strongly urged to attend the week-long national programs of leadership training, where a much more intensive period can be devoted to worldview perspectives as well as skills. Clergy training and advanced leadership training are typically conducted in shorter three-day sessions. Participation in these residential training programs helps construct a shared collective identity around organizing in the Alinsky tradition. Beginning organizers receive a more intensive program of socialization through mentoring by senior organizers, usually on a weekly basis. A volunteer leader in an organization is making a big commitment, taking a week off work and paying for travel and the workshop. Although member organizations often assist low-income leaders, and attendees are urged to raise money from friends and supporters, there are always some out-of-pocket expenses to be met. Attending week-long workshops is an indicator of the degree of commitment community organizations obtain from their core leadership.

One criticism that regularly surfaces regarding training seems to apply to all the major CBCO networks: the programs have gotten stale. The basic IAF curriculum dates back to the 1970s, for example, with little effort to systematically update the material. Although each new trainer is encouraged to bring his or her own examples to the various segments of training, the lineup of topics has not changed much, nor have the common themes and illustrations. Thucydides' "Melian Dialogue," mentioned above in the discussion of "the world as it is," is one example that has been used since Alinsky himself led the training. Trainers have made little use of video resources or other advances in technology, a deficiency also evident in the only recently developed contemporary organizational websites. The attitude of some of the long-time network leaders and trainers reminds one of the chorus of the song "Give Me That Old Time Religion," modified to "It was good for Saul Alinsky, and it's good enough for me."

A strong emphasis on these elements constructs and maintains an organizing subculture that is characteristic of the Alinsky tradition. Independent community organizations, and groups affiliated with networks from other traditions, use many of the items from the organizer's toolbox described in the next chapter, sharing techniques with the Alinsky tradition, without absorbing the worldview that accompanies it.

4

Tools of the Trade

In addition to the concepts and perspectives covered in Chapter 3, a blend of tools, skills, and tactics is also characteristic of (although not exclusive to) community organizing in the Alinsky tradition. The tools include one-on-ones, cutting issues from problems, and campaigns with a research–action–evaluation cycle. Although tactics may range from direct action to sitting down to talk with public officials, a successful campaign will likely require negotiating a final agreement. Skills needed by leaders to build powerful organizations include running effective meetings, agitation, power analysis, strategic planning and analysis, and fundraising. This chapter will present two case studies to illustrate strategic analysis and the public meeting.

Tools

One-on-Ones

The best organizing is based on public relationships. Ed Chambers says his greatest contribution has been the use of the relational meeting to build the foundations of broad-based community organizations:

> Modern IAF defines the relational meeting as an encounter that is face-to-face – one-to-one – for the purpose of exploring the development

of a public relationship. You're searching for talent, energy, insight, and relationships. . . . A solid relational meeting brings up stories that reveal people's deepest commitments and the experiences that give rise to them. In fact, the most important thing that happens in good relational meetings is the telling of stories that open a window into the passions that animate people to act. (Chambers 2004: 44–5)

Gamaliel clergy caucus leader Dennis Jacobsen puts it this way:

The one-on-one interview is the primary tool of organizing. A good organizer continually does one-on-ones and trains leaders to do the same. . . . On one level, a one-on-one is as natural as a conversation over a backyard fence or with a fellow passenger on an airplane. On another level it is skilled, artful, intentional, and focused. The one-on-one interview is a means of initiating or building a relationship. . . . We can only come to understand [someone] as we learn something about his or her childhood, family, job, education, faith, church, politics, hobbies, disappointments, dreams, anger, ambition. . . . At its heart, organizing is about relationships, not issues. (Jacobsen 2001: 59–60)

The purpose, then, of the one-on-one conversations is fourfold: to build a relationship with a person; to understand that person's motivation and self-interest; to create clarity about values; and to get information (Hart 2001: 105–7). These conversations produce the best results when the interviewer has the courage and curiosity to ask questions that evoke stories revealing a person's values, interests, and commitments – not questions that evoke a "yes" or "no" answer. Asking "why?" can also provide clarity.

As Gamaliel senior organizer Mary Gonzales points out, the interviewer is looking for a person's life experience, self-interest, values, ability to take risks, skills and talents, anger, and beauty. Also important is whether the person is relational – has organizational memberships, and circles of friends and followers. Don't judge, don't preach in a one-on-one conversation. Be curious and listen intently.

There are a number of conventions for one-on-ones, Alinsky style. Appointments are made in advance, for a 30-minute meeting. The person setting up the meeting asks the questions, taking no notes during the meeting (but makes notes afterwards). The interviewer keeps to an 80–20 rule: talk no more than 20 percent of the time; listen for 80 percent of the conversation.

An important outcome of one-on-ones may be establishing a public relationship with the other person – not the private relationships one has with a family member or close friend, but the mutual commitment to the civic goals of the community organization. Only with that public relationship can people hold one another accountable for the activities of the organization and agitate one another to do more and do better in defining and realizing one's self-interest. Relationships build community among participants in the organization's work and are the grounding for the organization's power (Hart 2001: 73–5).

Cutting Issues from Problems

Social problems are frequently manifestations of large-scale troubles within a society: high unemployment, poverty, increasing inequality, lack of affordable housing, substandard education, dropout rates from high schools, lack of affordable health care, militarism, and on and on. It would be difficult to imagine how a community organization could make much headway in solving such complex dilemmas.

The Alinsky organizing tradition has emphasized reducing these overwhelming problems into manageable issues – known as "cutting issues from problems." As Alinsky wrote, "An issue is something you can do something about. . . . Organizations are built on issues that are specific, immediate, and realizable" (Alinsky 1972: 119–20).

Organizer Susan Shaw defines the challenge as follows: "A good issue is measurable (you will know whether you succeeded or not), has a short time-line, has a clear target, and is winnable. In addition, it's in people's hearts and minds, it's based on relationships, and it helps develop leaders." Another mnemonic refers to the "SMART" criteria: specific, measurable, attainable, relevant, and timely.

Some critics of the Alinsky organizing approach have argued

that the "winnability" criterion limits the group's objectives to minor local issues, and prevents it from ever getting around to tackling those matters really crucial to survival in declining communities. They argue for more visionary goals to campaigns, with the belief that they may not be successful this year, or even next year, but they will triumph in the long run, and make a real difference in people's lives.

Organizer Mike Miller makes the case for "winnability" as enabling larger steps toward more complex issues:

> You cannot build a powerful movement for transformative change, and the powerful organizations that are required to sustain such a movement, without victories along the way. The victories are essential to convince people of the efficacy of collective action and to sustain themselves in it; to invest their time, talent and money in such a movement; to see it as a vehicle to express deeply held values like democracy, freedom, equality, security, community, and justice; to understand it as a means to defend things most important to them – their personhood, families, friends, neighborhoods, work, and income. . . . Victories allow initial participants to go home and tell their families, friends, co-congregants, fellow workers and neighbors, "Look what we did. We can do even more with more people." (Morales and Miller 2011: 51–2)

In response and in partial agreement with Miller, activist and artist Ricardo Levins Morales writes:

> To move our deepest dreams from the unwinnable column into the winnable, we need to begin fighting for them while they still seem out of reach. . . . One reason we focus on immediate victories is because our battered communities need to re-learn that winning is even conceivable. This need is less in places with strong movement cultures, where past victories are retained in the collective memory. (Morales and Miller 2011: 83)

Campaigns: The Research–Action–Evaluation Cycle

Sociologist Charles Tilly defines a campaign as "a sustained, organized public effort making collective claims on target authorities"

73

(Tilly 2004: 3). Community organizations develop leaders and build power through issue campaigns that follow a cycle of research, action, and evaluation.

Research   Having settled on one or more issues, an issue task force begins the research phase by identifying all the people who have a stake in the issue, and especially identifying the person, or body of people (such as a city council), with the power to give you what you want. They could become the "target" of the action. Task force members set up interviews with persons who can provide information to help assess the details of the situation, or perhaps the decision-makers themselves to find out their interests and position on the issue. When two or more task force members meet with an official or expert outside the organization, sometimes that is called a "power one-on-one." In general, team members will meet before the appointment to assign roles, allocate questions to the various members of the team, appoint a recorder, and consider their overall strategy for the meeting. Members work to establish control of the meeting by keeping to their questions, refusing to be diverted from their "script." After the meeting the team members immediately gather again to evaluate the meeting and whether the interview went as planned, and whether they got the information they needed.

Veteran organizer Shel Trapp from National People's Action has some useful guidelines for research: you don't need all the information for a whole campaign before starting to take action. You only need enough information to be confident at a first meeting. Trapp's basic assumption is that "research is not a security blanket. It is a weapon in the organization's arsenal and should be used as such" (Trapp 1979: 2). A couple of well-prepared and well-evaluated interviews should be enough to get most grassroots leaders past questioning their competence ("Who, me a researcher?") to do this work.

Action   IAF senior organizer Michael Gecan offers a basic definition of an action: ". . . when more than one person, focused on a particular issue, engages a person in power directly responsible for that issue, for the purpose of getting a reaction" (Gecan 2002: 50–1). Taking action is the breath and the lifeblood of the organization. Alinsky noted: "Organizations need action as an individual needs oxygen. The cessation of action brings death to the organization through factionalism and inaction, through dialogues and conferences that are actually a form of rigor mortis rather than life" (Alinsky 1972: 120). He also observed that "most lessons of life are learned in and through action" (Alinsky 1989: 213). Actions should begin by personalizing (but not demonizing) and polarizing the issue. When you get a positive result, you need to relax the tension and depersonalize and depolarize (Chambers 2004: 84–6). And as Alinsky noted, "The real action is in the enemy's reaction" (Alinsky 1972: 136). By which he meant that the target's response to your action is the crucial element in the event, and determines your next action. A plan of action necessarily raises the question of tactics, a subject that we address below.

Evaluation In the world of community organizing, anything worth doing is worth evaluating. "You are just a pile of undigested happenings," Alinsky once told one of his organizers (Chambers 2004: 87). A quick evaluation is conducted after every meeting and every action. How did the designated individuals perform their roles? Did we stick to our plan? What was the reaction of the target? Were any media present? Any glitches? How are you feeling about the action? What can we do better next time?

In the course of a campaign, there may be many actions, with different tactics used as appropriate. Each action will be followed by evaluation. Additional research also might be conducted if necessary. At the end of a campaign a more detailed evaluation should be done, with lessons learned.

Tactics

Tactics, generally speaking, are skillful methods used to gain an end during an engagement with an opponent. Alinsky summarized: "Tactics means doing what you can with what you have" (Alinsky 1972: 126). Reading some of the more outlandish stories of Alinsky tactics – most of which never really happened – one might conclude that acting in his spirit means thinking up the most novel outrageous stunt, which will be followed by immediate capitulation by the target of the action. It's surprising, then, to read Alinsky's advice from the conclusion of his last book, *Rules for Radicals*: "Tactics must begin within the experience of the middle class, accepting their aversion to rudeness, vulgarity, and conflict. Start them easy, don't scare them off" (Alinsky 1972: 195).

Aaron Schutz and Marie Sandy list some criteria for a good tactic:

- puts pressure on a target;
- includes a specific demand;
- gets large numbers of people involved;
- educates your members and develops leaders (Schutz and Sandy 2011: 260).

Other Alinsky rules for tactics include:

- "Never go outside the experience of your people."
- "Whenever possible go outside of the experience of the enemy."
- "Make the enemy live up to their own book of rules."
- "A good tactic is one that your people enjoy" (Alinsky 1972: 126–8).

Negotiation

In the real world ("the world as it is") no one gets everything they want. A community organization has to recognize the need to negotiate. A position of "Here are our demands, no negotiations!" is for moral purists who are happy to go down in self-righteous defeat (Trapp 1976: 21). Shel Trapp has excellent suggestions for the critical negotiating phase of a campaign. As he points out,

"This is where you either bring home the bacon or lose it" (Trapp 1986: 22).

The tactics of your organization have got the attention of your target, and you have been invited to present your concerns and proposals. Seldom does a target simply capitulate and grant demands without discussion. An organization must be ready for negotiations. Always negotiate from a position of strength, and only negotiate with the person with the power to grant your proposal. Know the facts from your research, and be prepared to illustrate them with stories. Assign a chief negotiator and roles for the other members of your negotiating team. Negotiate specifics, one point at a time. Know what your bottom line is. Get the agreement in writing, signed by both parties. Make a plan for follow-up and accountability (Trapp 1986: 22–4).

Skills

Running Effective Meetings

How its meetings are run says a great deal about an organization – whether it respects people's time, whether it wants to be inviting to people from all walks of life, and to what extent it is serious about getting its business done. Some practical tips for good meetings that get people coming back:

- hold only those meetings that are necessary for making decisions;
- distribute a timed, written agenda before the meeting;
- start and stop on time;
- avoid esoteric rules and practices that leave some people feeling like outsiders (an example from Occupy Wall Street: "twinkling" fingers to indicate agreement or as a substitute for applause) (Pierce 1984: 122–7).

A useful maxim heard at a Gamaliel training: "Any meeting lasting longer than two hours isn't a meeting, it's a retreat." Keep meetings short and to the point. It's surprising how strong a positive impression this can leave with people who have endured too many rambling, pointless meetings.

Agitation

Agitation, in the sense used in community organizing, is a tool to challenge leaders to act out of their values and self-interest, to be accountable, to grow, and to contribute their best to the success of their organization. As organizer Philip Cryan notes, "Agitation can move a person from identifying a problem they wish were solved toward deciding to take an active role in solving it" (Cryan n.d. [ca. 2012]: 9). Sociologist Robert Kleidman (2005) notes that potential leaders are "challenged and supported to examine their histories to uncover anger at injustices that appear personal but upon examination have systemic roots, to explore and clarify their values, and to make a serious commitment to personal development through organizing" (Kleidman 2005: 41). Organizers set out to discover what is great about potential leaders, and confront and challenge them to behave in those ways. As political scientist Heidi Swarts writes, "The nominal purpose of all this confrontation is to evoke a reaction that agitates participants out of passivity and into active involvement" (Swarts 2008: 16). Agitation can be disconcerting to people unused to being called upon to take responsibility for living out their professed values and interests. If first encountered in a one-week workshop, where relationships may be minimal, agitation can put some people on the defensive. Nevertheless, when undertaken in a spirit of care and love, and within a developed relationship, it can be most effective. Networks differ in their reliance on agitation, with Gamaliel noted for a strong emphasis and PICO for taking a "kinder, gentler" approach.

Power Analysis

A crucial question for an organization to explore for any emerging issue is: whose interests would put them in opposition to you, and whose interests might make them allies? Once the parties of interest are identified, the question becomes: how powerful, how influential are these individuals? Persons with power could be business owners or executives: leaders in manufacturing, banking, agriculture, and construction. They may be leaders in the professions: lawyers, doctors, and architects. They may be owners of media that reach substantial sectors of the population: TV and radio stations, newspapers, and so on. They may include executives of chambers of commerce, civic associations, members of the boards of the local community foundation, or other important charities. Some may be significant donors to the arts, to private hospitals, or to colleges and universities.

Elected officials are people with power: city council members, mayors, county supervisors, judges, state legislators, governors, US Congressional members and Senators. They may be long-term appointed administrators: from city managers to cabinet secretaries.

The academic analysis of community power typically uses one of three methodologies to determine who has power: reputational (asking people of influence who has power in the community), positional (who holds positions of potential economic, social, or political power), and case studies of who influenced specific decisions. The pluralist view holds that there are many sets of interests to any specific public issues, and in a democratic society all can organize to defend their interests. The result will be the best compromise that can be arrived at. Critics of pluralism argue that economic inequality stacks the deck in favor of wealth and social cohesion among an economic elite, which has more power and will commonly prevail.

The danger of projecting a solid, impenetrable community power structure is reducing elected and appointed officials to mere "instruments" of private interests. A more sophisticated analysis would see government reflecting the present state of the conflict among, as Alinsky put it, the "haves," the "have nots," and the "have a little, want more group" (Sanders 1970: 69). Political scientist Peter Dreier points out the importance of avoiding the type of power structure research that leads to "the dead-end of cynicism, fatalism, and apathy." He argues for a form of "power struggle" research that is "neither fatalistic nor utopian" (Dreier 1975: 242).

Classic studies in the field include Floyd Hunter's *Community Power Structure* (1953 – he coined the term) and C. Wright Mills' *The Power Elite* (1959). Hunter used the reputational method to study the powers that be in "Southern City" (Atlanta, GA), and Mills took a national-level view of powerful positions in politics, business, labor, and the military. The liberal pluralist view is defended by Robert Dahl in his case study of New Haven, *Who Governs?* (1961).

G. William Domhoff (2005) followed Mills in developing a class-domination theory of power. On the local level, Domhoff sees a specific segment of the dominant class, which he calls the "growth coalition," holding the greatest share of power. Domhoff's model has been applied to Santa Rosa in Sonoma County, California, by James Wilkinson (2010) in a study of control of the Santa Rosa City Council from 2000 to 2010. He sees the "growth machine" of developers and business owners having dominated local politics in all but two of the past 30 years, but sees increasing power in the emerging "progressive coalition," including environmentalists, affordable housing advocates, historic preservationists, and some elements of labor.

Strategic Planning

Organizations are constantly changing. Leaders drop out for any number of reasons: they get new jobs, move away, marry, divorce, get ill, die. Organizing staff come and go. New groups and congregations join a broad-based community organization; old member groups decline and fall away. Member groups may have financial crises and can't pay dues. National events impact organizations: the economy goes into recession; elections bring into office a different political majority with new economic and social policies. The world is constantly in flux; change is the only constant.

How does an organization cope with the inevitability of change? The answer of the business, government, and nonprofit worlds is strategic planning. Typically strategic planning involves an internal organizational analysis and an external scan of the environment in which the organization operates. Most community organizations use a simple formula, termed a SWOT analysis, standing for strengths, weaknesses, opportunities, and threats. The first two points review the strengths and weaknesses of the organization itself, and the other two the opportunities and threats in the external environment.

As an example, the North Bay Organizing Project (NBOP), toward the end of its third year of public visibility, concluded that its strengths included a diverse organizational membership comprising a variety of congregations, unions, and other groups representing environmentalists, immigrants, and labor advocates. Weaknesses included a lack of Catholic parishes as members, and a dues structure that provided too small a proportion of the budget, leaving the organization too dependent on foundation grants and fundraising activities. Scanning the external environment, the NBOP had gained a good reputation in the community for its campaigning on immigrant rights, its development of young Latino leaders, and its work on transportation equity and neighborhood development. As a Gamaliel network affiliate, the NBOP faces the threat of competition from an older but now mostly dormant IAF affiliate, the North Bay Sponsoring Committee, that makes occasional efforts to revive its local supporters. It also faces a strong PICO network in California, which has not yet tried to cultivate an affiliate in the North Bay.

The NBOP did not win its campaign supporting a November 2012 ballot measure that would have shifted from at-large to district elections for the Santa Rosa City Council. Nevertheless, its leadership on the issue had made a number of new allies and positioned the NBOP to help push the city of Santa Rosa to annex an "island" of unincorporated land entirely surrounded by the city that contains the homes of some 6,500 residents, a majority of whom are Latinos. The organization recognized that it would need to upgrade its capacity to register new voters, engage them in civic action between elections, and mobilize its volunteers to get out the vote on election days.

Tools of the Trade

Strategic Analysis: A Neglected Dimension?

Although strategic planning is a skill taught as part of an annual projection of work in the year ahead, strategic analysis can be a deeper look at the social, economic, and political trends that can impact the longer-range work of community organizations and networks. Such analysis may alert leaders and organizers to barriers to progress as well as to "windows of political opportunity," on the national, state, and local level. Emerging splits and rivalries among opponents may present opportunities that call for action. Disasters – natural or man-made – may draw attention to issues that need to be addressed. Demographic trends may sustain hope for progress if clearly understood: an example is the likely emergence of a political majority in the United States favoring Democrats over Republicans in the next couple of decades, as outlined by John Judis and Ruy Teixeira (2004). As the following example shows, labor and civil rights leader A. Philip Randolph was one of the shrewdest organizers to take advantage of his moments of political opportunity.

Case Study: A. Philip Randolph Wins Demands from Two Presidents

Randolph's Brotherhood of Sleeping Car Porters never had more than 15,000 members at its peak in the 1940s, all of whom worked for one corporation: the Pullman Company. Many of the members had little formal education, yet the pay was good, and porters were highly respected in African American communities. Porters traveled around the country, and played an important role bringing news from the North to the South (and distributing such black newspapers as the *Chicago Defender, Pittsburgh Courier*, and New York's *Amsterdam News*). With this small but significant organization behind him, Randolph negotiated some remarkable gains of benefit to millions of African Americans and other minorities and women as well.

Randolph was a master of the strategic use of power at moments when the windows of political opportunity were open. In 1941, as President Franklin Roosevelt was preparing the country for a likely war with Nazi Germany, Randolph demanded the President end discrimination against blacks and other minorities in defense industries and in federal government employment. He threatened a march on Washington by thousands of black people if Roosevelt failed to issue an executive order. Not wanting to be seen by the rest of the world as discriminating against minorities at a time when he was proclaiming the United States to be a beacon of liberty, Roosevelt gave in and signed Executive Order 8802 ending discrimination by defense contractors and establishing a Committee on Fair Employment Practices. Randolph called off the planned march (Anderson 1972: 241–61).

After the Second World War, Randolph staged a confrontation with Harry Truman, who had succeeded to the Presidency upon Roosevelt's death in 1945. Truman was running for election to a second term in 1948 under difficult circumstances. The Democratic Party had split, with its left wing following Secretary of Agriculture and former Vice President Henry Wallace into the Progressive Party. The right wing left with Strom Thurman and his States Rights Party. Republican Thomas Dewey, governor of New York, looked to be a certain winner. In the context of a growing Cold War with the Soviet Union, Truman was supporting a call for universal military training and reinstating a military draft. Meeting with the President, Randolph threatened to lead a boycott of the military by blacks if Truman didn't issue an executive order desegregating the armed forces. Although he was outraged, equating Randolph's threat with treason, Truman nevertheless issued Executive Order 9981 before the election (Anderson 1972: 274–82; Pfeffer 1990: 133–68). Truman won a narrow victory over Dewey, surprising many (including the *Chicago Daily Tribune*, with its famous headline announcing "Dewey Defeats Truman"). The black vote proved decisive for Truman in winning California, Illinois, and Ohio (McAdam 1982: 81), thus providing his margin of victory in the Electoral College.

Randolph finally saw his vision of a march realized with the August 1963 March on Washington for Jobs and Freedom, at which Martin Luther King, Jr. gave his famous "I Have a Dream" speech. Randolph's prestige in the African American community gave him the standing to bring together the often feuding leaders of the primarily black civil rights organizations: Roy Wilkins of the NAACP, Whitney Young of the National Urban League, Martin Luther King, Jr. of the SCLC, James Farmer of CORE, and John Lewis of SNCC. Important white allies supporting the March included Walter Reuther of the United Auto Workers and Arnold Aronson of the Leadership Conference on Civil Rights (Barber 2002: 141–78).

Fundraising

Community organizers like to say that power has two sources: organized money and organized people. Corporations and the economic elite have the edge in organized money, but – potentially at least – communities should have the advantage in organized people. Of course, community organizations also need money, but from whom that money is raised has an important impact on the organization's freedom to act.

The more money an organization can raise from its own members and supporters, the greater independence and power it will have. Community organizing in the Alinsky tradition rejects accepting funding from government at any level – local, state, or federal. The experience of ACORN alone, which we discuss in Chapter 5, should make clear the hazards of substantial dependence on federal grants or contracts. Ideally, private foundation support should also be rejected, but it is not realistic for most organizations to meet their budgets without some foundation support.

One rule of thumb is to strive for 25 percent of income from each of:

- organizational membership dues;
- individual contributions, major donors;
- grassroots fundraising activities;
- foundation grants.

For those community organizations that have organizational members (congregation-based or broad-based), the dues from member organizations should provide the base of support for their budget. Contributions from individuals who are members of member organizations or supporters from the community are another important source of core support. These contributions can be made as annual gifts, contributions during major public meetings, or monthly charges to a credit card or bank account. Pledges can be solicited during an annual period devoted to individual giving.

Grassroots fundraising can be based on special events – an annual dinner can sell tables of eight or ten seats as well as individual tickets. Local businesses can be solicited for support, and gifts acknowledged in ad books printed for the event. Variations on the special event can include dances with DJs or live music, luncheons, and receptions. Think big: the Pilsen Neighbors Community Council in Chicago runs a four-day street fair, the Fiesta del Sol, which draws 1.3 million people to the largest Latino festival in the Midwest. Net proceeds from the festival – $300,000 in recent years – provide a substantial portion of the organization's budget for the year. Several excellent books on grassroots fundraising are available to spark your imagination and give you confidence that you can do it (see Flanagan 1982, 2002; Klein 2011; Seltzer 2002).

Research on community organizations and fundraising suggests that access to religious and secular foundation donors is enhanced by participation in one of the national or regional networks. In a survey of community organizations that survived from the 1990s to the late 2000s, Edward Walker and John McCarthy found that the groups had succeeded in reallocating substantial amounts of money into employment, education, health, and public services to previously underserved communities. Members of these organizations have been empowered to participate in the political arena, promoting social justice on such issues as immigration, policing, and home ownership. Moreover, they have had considerable impact with modest levels of funding and staff. Public engagement often includes lobbying legislators; rallies and demonstrations tend to be preferred to more disruptive tactics like civil disobedience. The organizations surveyed had a diverse funding stream, including foundations (37 percent), member dues (13 percent), individual gifts (10 percent), and fundraisers (6 percent) – still a way to go to the ideal, but promising (Walker and McCarthy 2012).

Public Meetings

A distinctive tactic of the Alinsky tradition of community organizing is the public meeting, also known as an "accountability session," in which a large crowd of supporters is assembled and the organization's program is presented to the public. Political officials are asked whether or not they support particular parts within their scope of authority. Public meetings are best understood as a form of political theater. All aspects of the program are carefully rehearsed, and all the speeches are scripted and timed – there are seldom any surprises in the events.

The format of the public meeting is more or less standard across the various networks. Meetings begin and end with a prayer. A diverse group of leaders run the meeting, make presentations, and question public officials. The staff organizers do not speak and generally stay out of sight. After the conclusion of the meeting, everyone involved in planning and presenting the meeting gathers for an evaluation (Hart 2001: 100–2). (For a detailed guide to holding accountability sessions, see Bobo et al. 2010: 79–96.)

An example is the first public meeting of the North Bay Organizing Project in Sonoma County, California, held in October 2011. The NBOP had held its first issues assembly seven months before, in March, at which it identified two issue areas it would work on over the next half-year, and created two task forces to work on them. First, the Immigration Task Force would research the police and sheriff's departments' impounding of automobiles of undocumented immigrants and the deportation of many who were arrested and booked for lack of satisfactory identifying papers. Second, the Transportation Equity and Neighborhood Development Task Force would research three interconnected issues. The first was the Station Area Plans along a developing passenger rail line known as the SMART (Sonoma–Marin Area Rail Transit) train and pathway. These plans are important for the zones they allocate to affordable housing, businesses, and parks. The second issue was the redevelopment vision for a mostly empty shopping center in Roseland, a heavily Latino, low-income, unincorporated enclave within southwest Santa Rosa. The third issue concerned a proposed bicycle and pedestrian bridge, spanning Highway 101, which cuts through the center of Santa Rosa. Success would be to win the support of the Santa Rosa City Council to fund a required study, the next step toward constructing the bridge. In the public meeting the organization would report its progress on these issues.

Sociologist Charles Tilly argues that social movements have three defining characteristics: they conduct campaigns, they utilize a social movement repertoire of tactics, and they engage in displays of their worthiness, unity, numbers, and commitment (WUNC) (Tilly 2004: 4). The NBOP public meeting confirmed his observation that social movement organizations believe they will benefit from making public representations of their WUNC.

Case Study: The NBOP's First Public Meeting

The afternoon was unusually warm for late October in northern California. On such a sunny Sunday you would expect families to drive out to the Sonoma County coast or have a picnic along the Russian River or among the vineyards and wineries of Dry Creek or the Alexander Valley.

Instead, people were filing into the Santa Rosa High School Auditorium, a structure separate from the classroom building next door, but constructed in the same classic Brick Gothic style that once made the school a popular site for Hollywood to film teen movies. The crowd was there to attend the first public meeting of the North Bay Organizing Project.

Outside, in front of the auditorium, young men wearing white shirts and black pants and women in white blouses and black skirts or slacks from the MEChA clubs (Movimiento Estudiantil Chicano de Aztlan; see Gómez-Quiñones 1990: 118–24; Muñoz 1989: 75–6) at Santa Rosa Junior College and Sonoma State University were directing new arrivals to registration tables for the various organizations that formed the NBOP: the Committee for Immigrant Rights, the Redwood Forest Friends (Quaker) Meeting, the Graton Day Labor Center, Sonoma County Conservation Action, the Living Wage Coalition, the Sonoma County Council of MoveOn, and others.

A veteran reporter and columnist for the daily *Press Democrat* reflected on the participants: "This was not your usual public meeting audience of consultants, interest groups and government-watchers. This was families and working people and students, Latinos and blacks, old people and young people. It was a diverse crowd that represented the entire community – definitely different from politics as usual" (Coursey 2011).

Inside the auditorium, the ground floor holding 650 people had filled, and latecomers were climbing the stairs to the balcony, from which banners of the member groups were displayed. The atmosphere in the auditorium, the *Press Democrat* reported, "had the feel of part victorious political rally, part community party, and part tent revival" (Johnson 2011). "One elected official," the *Press Democrat's* columnist noted, "walked into the auditorium, looked around and whistled his astonishment at the size of the crowd. 'This is impressive,' he said. 'I wonder if they all vote'" (Coursey 2011).

The meeting was called to order about 10 minutes after the appointed starting time of 3 p.m. by the president of the Organizing Project, a 30-year-old Mexican American, the son of immigrants, who works as the lead organizer for the Graton Day Labor Center. After a brief welcome, presented in English and then in Spanish (all of the afternoon's proceedings were bilingual), he called the roll of the member organizations that were seated together on the ground floor of the auditorium, giving each group an opportunity to stand and cheer. Toward the end of the roll call, a dozen mostly young people from Occupy Santa Rosa, formed just three weeks before, entered the auditorium with signs and banners, after marching the mile and a half up Mendocino Avenue from their encampment at City Hall. As they made their way to a section reserved for guests, the audience rose and gave them a standing ovation. That was the one truly spontaneous, unscripted event of the afternoon.

After a lengthy opening prayer offered by a Pomo Indian spiritual leader, the NBOP president introduced the invited elected officials in attendance: three of the five county supervisors, a mayor and council members from three cities, and a state Assemblyman. Representatives of the county sheriff and police chiefs from three cities were also present.

A brief statement of the Organizing Project's vision for the region was read by a retired professor, a member of the NBOP's leadership council.

> We develop leadership from our member organizations and break down the dividing lines of race, class, gender, and geography. We strengthen the bonds among our diverse communities, develop deeper relationships with one another, lift up leadership, engage in public life, organize, and build our collective power! We are not prepared to abandon the American dream of a democratic and just society. We support jobs that pay a living wage [*cheers from the audience*], healthy neighborhoods with affordable housing [*more cheers*], equal access

to education for all students [*cheers again*], and public transportation that serves all people [*cheers*]. We work to build a culture of civic engagement in which all may find their voices and all may be heard. And we invite all who share this vision to join with us!

Two women – one the Latina vice-president of the NBOP, and the other an Anglo woman social service worker – related their intensely personal and emotionally moving stories of their passage from oppression to power.

Then it was time to begin reports on the actions undertaken by the two Task Forces established at the issues assembly seven months before. The big news was the work of the Immigration Task Force. The county sheriff and the city police chiefs had agreed to accept the *matricula consular* card issued by the Mexican Consulate as proof of identity.

A young Latina woman, herself now a US citizen, described what happened to her brother, who had been stopped a month earlier by local police while driving home from work. Although he produced a Mexican *matricula* card as evidence of his identity, he was arrested, booked at the jail, and fingerprinted. His prints were sent to Immigration and Customs Enforcement (popularly known as ICE). Despite his having no outstanding warrants or felony offenses on record, he was promptly deported back to Mexico.

The young woman introduced her 11-year-old daughter, who had been standing at her side. Three years earlier, the students in her third-grade class were given the assignment of writing a letter to the new President. The girl began in a nervous but clear voice:

Growing up with an undocumented parent is very difficult. I had to wonder what would happen if my mom was stopped by the police and ended up deported. How would I be reunited with her? This is when my third-grade teacher asked us to write a letter to President Obama with a request. I knew right away what to ask. And this is my letter:

"Dear President Obama, I am a third grader. I am writing this letter to tell you that I'm happy you are our new President, and I have a request for you. I want you to give papers to all immigrants so they can get licenses, and they don't get deported. That way all families can be together. Sincerely, Alma O."

After enthusiastic applause for her daughter, the young woman invited the assistant sheriff and the Santa Rosa police chief to come to the stage. "Will you accept the Mexican consular card as a valid ID?" she asked the assistant sheriff. "Claro," he replied in Spanish. The audience rose and gave a prolonged ovation of applause and cheers. Once the assistant sheriff had elaborated his office's position, the Santa Rosa police captain answered "Yes" to the same question, and spoke briefly.

A representative of the Mexican consulate in San Francisco was invited to the stage. She commended the NBOP for its work on this issue, and promised to work with the organization to issue more *matricula* cards to Mexican citizens residing in the North Bay.

The Transportation Equity and Neighborhood Development Task Force had researched its three interconnected issues: the station area plans along the SMART train line, the redevelopment of the shopping center in Roseland, and the proposed bicycle and pedestrian bridge spanning Highway 101.

Research meetings with public officials revealed that an important step needed to be taken immediately by the Santa Rosa City Council to continue toward construction of the bridge. Caltrans (the California Department of Transportation) required an impact study that needed to be funded by the City of Santa Rosa. Aside from one councilman who was an avid bicycle supporter, in a tight budgetary year the majority of the council did not appear to favor funding the study. In addition, the "Bicycle Bridge," as it was called, was being portrayed as the exclusive concern of a local professional elite with their Spandex racing suits and their $3,000 carbon-fiber bicycles. Nonetheless, the Task Force decided it might be able to win on the issue of funding the study.

The first order of business was to reframe the "Bicycle Bridge" as the "Community Connector Bridge." East of Highway 101 are the wealthy parts of town, the hospitals, the City and County offices, and the Junior College. Speaking for the Task Force, a young woman from the Student Senate of the Santa Rosa Junior College argued that the bridge was a matter of social justice for Santa Rosa: "We are a deeply divided community. Highway 101 separates us by race and class," she said. "The bridge needs to be a priority." The *Press Democrat* observer noted, "As she listed the benefits – commerce, jobs, economic stimulus, safety, mobility, the environment – the crowd began to chant: 'Connect us now! Connect us now! Connect us now!' Funny, but it felt like a connection already had been made" (Coursey 2011).

The members present from the Santa Rosa City Council and the state Assembly representative were called to the stage and asked if they would support the study for the Community Connector Bridge. One by one they answered "Yes!" The accountability section of the program was over – and none too soon as the meeting was now running late and people were beginning to leave.

The NBOP treasurer came quickly to the podium and made an appeal for "investments" in the Organizing Project, and a collection was gathered. The fundraising pitch was the meeting's final item of business. The closing prayer was offered by a former Episcopal minister now part of the Quaker meeting. That wrapped up, the NBOP president thanked the crowd for coming and adjourned the meeting.

As the remaining crowd filed out, the planning committee and the leadership council members gathered at the front of the auditorium for the evaluation. The two staff organizers, who played no visible role in the public face of the meeting and were glimpsed only occasionally along the side of the room, emerged to lead the evaluation as the auditorium emptied. They were joined by Mary Gonzales of the Gamaliel Foundation staff, their consultant to the NBOP. The NBOP leadership were pleased that the crowd was substantial and relieved that they got through the performance with no major glitches. But Gonzales was not about to let them be complacent. The program ran way past the time planned, she pointed out. Speeches were too long, which was multiplied by the need for translation. Speakers should have been better briefed and rehearsed. Leaders should have adjusted the program when it became clear that time was running short. People were leaving by the time contributions were solicited. Registration was chaotic and took too much time. Softening a bit, Gonzales congratulated the group for a good showing and a spirited audience for a first public meeting. Everyone agreed they would be better prepared for the next event. The newspaper accounts the next day were very complimentary, and all in all people felt very good about the event and the accomplishments that had been made in only half a year. The *Press Democrat* columnist captured the meeting's significance: "If you were paying close attention," he wrote, "you may have felt the balance of political power shift ever so slightly this week in Santa Rosa" (Coursey 2011).

5

New Networks Innovate

The IAF approach of organizing religious congregations into powerful local and regional networks has been taken up by other organizations, two of which, PICO and Gamaliel, are national in scope. A third, the Direct Action and Research Training Center (DART), is better described as regional, with affiliates in Florida and the Southeast. Several of these networks' leaders got their start with the IAF, or with other Alinsky associates, such as Tom Gaudette. Other networks related to the Alinsky tradition, but one step further removed, include National People's Action, USAction, and ACORN. This chapter will describe some of the innovative contributions to community organizing practice made by the newer networks, and explore what gives organizations the resilience to survive internal scandal and external attack. We will make use of Virginia Hine's SPIN analysis of networked SMOs and John McCarthy and Mayer Zald's analysis of SMOs and their relationships to one another.

Zald and McCarthy develop an economic metaphor that considers all the SMOs of a similar sort as located within a social movement industry (SMI). If SMOs in the same SMI compete for resources from the same limited number of sources (grant funds from liberal foundations, say), the SMOs can be expected to be competitive toward one another. If they can manage to develop distinct specialties through "product differentiation," the degree of competition could be reduced. Similarly, varied geographic focus could reduce competition and enhance cooperation. On the other hand, overlapping "turf" is likely to increase competitive-ness. This becomes clear in the case of the national community organizing networks (Zald and McCarthy 1987: 161–80).

A central trend in community organizing over the past two decades is the expansion of spatial scope from a neighborhood or section of a city, to the regional or metropolitan area, and beyond to the state, or even national, level. This evolution raises the question: should a mature community organization, as part of a network, be able to embrace each of these levels – local, regional, state, or national – as a focus of actions for change? Can community organizing take on policy goals of state or national significance without losing its soul of rootedness in a community of people with deep relationships?

And what happens then to independent local organizations not linked to a regional or national network? "Training intermediar-ies" (Delgado 1994), from the Midwest Academy to the Center for Third World Organizing, have been particularly important for independent community organizations to keep up with best prac-tices and train their leaders and staff organizers. But independent organizations have to find their own allies and partners to have an impact on regional, state, and national policy issues.

The SPIN Model of Social Movement Networks

Virginia Hine's (1977) model of Segmented Polycentric Ideological Networks (SPIN) offers insights into the strengths and adaptabil-ity of nonprofit advocacy networks with national, state, and local structures. An anthropologist at the University of Miami, Hine did much of her work on social movements with fellow anthropologist Luther Gerlach of the University of Minnesota (e.g. Gerlach and Hine 1970). Hine argued that SPIN is the structure best suited for the survival and success of social movements.

"*Segmented*," in Hine's model, refers to the way in which an organization may have a national structure with semi-autonomous local groups and may also have state organizations for coordina-tion at that level. Several SMOs with active membership structures illustrate this concept. For example, the Sierra Club has 55 chapters in the United States (generally one to a state, although New England and the Dakotas are each covered by a single chapter, and California has 13), and within the chapters some 350 local groups, typically covering a county. The American Civil Liberties Union has 51 state affiliates, which in turn have chapters, typically representing a county. The community organizing networks have also developed state structures when they have enough affiliates: the IAF has Texas Interfaith representing its 10 affiliates in that state; PICO California represents 19 local affiliates; and Gamaliel has its Wisconsin affiliates linked in WISDOM. Being at least semi-autonomous, these organizational segments are potentially capable of self-sufficiency. This allows a national organization and its affiliates to survive a scandal or defection of a single local or cluster of locals – even a whole state – without the entire organization being undermined. Or in the reverse case, viable locals can disaffiliate from a discredited national leadership. In this chapter we will explore the usefulness of this concept in understanding how such groups as Citizen Action, ACORN, and National People's Action survived or collapsed as a result of external attacks or self-inflicted wounds.

"*Polycentric*" recalls that most social movements are composed of several major national organizations that may compete as well as cooperate. (Hines' original article uses the term "Polycephalous," i.e., multi-headed, but shifts to the more easily understood "Polycentric" in later references.) We've referred to four major congregation-based community organizing networks in the United States: the IAF, PICO, Gamaliel, and DART. The environmental movement, to take another example, has numerous national organizations, including groups with active members and chapters (such as the Sierra Club and the National Audubon Society) as well as staff-driven advocacy organizations (such as the Environmental Defense Fund, the Natural Resources Defense Council, EarthJustice, and the Wilderness Society). Some, like the National Wildlife Federation, have state affiliates with active members, and others, like the National Parks Conservation Association, offer opportunities for volunteer member participation. The organizations within a social movement have been conceptualized as existing within a "multi-organizational field" consisting not only of allied groups but also of opposing groups and interests (Rucht 2004).

"*Ideological*" is meant by Hine to indicate "a deep commitment to a very few basic tenets shared by all" (Hine 1977: 20). For community organizing, this might include such shared tenets as developing indigenous leaders; building powerful organizations that take on multiple issues; acting to make democracy a reality; and putting together broad-based organizations that include a variety of racial, ethnic, religious, and income groups. In a general sense, political scientist David Easton defines ideology as "articulated sets of ideals, ends and purposes which help the members of a system interpret the past, explain the present, and offer a vision of the future" (Easton 1968: 44). Radical critics of the Alinsky tradition fault its failure to develop an ideology in this robust sense (Fisher and Kling 1987).

"*Network*" suggests a web-like set of connections among organizations that minimizes hierarchy, and allows for multiple horizontal connections among groups. The network may have a center, but one that facilitates, by providing training and consultation, for example, rather than dominating the associated groups. Networks are composed of autonomous groups united by values and interests (Lipnack and Stamps 1986: 1–13). Networks offer community organizations access to ideas, information, and resources beyond those immediately available on the local scene. Staff of the network hubs can serve as the "connectors" that Malcolm Gladwell identifies as sources of social power, people we "rely on to give us access to opportunities and worlds to which we don't belong" (Gladwell 2000: 54). Networks offer the "power of weak ties."

PICO National Network

PICO provides an example of a network of CBCOs developing a statewide presence, and going on to apply its learning to have an impact on national policy. PICO was founded in 1972 in Oakland, California, by Jesuit priests John Baumann and Jerry Helfrich as the Oakland Training Institute. They changed its name to the Pacific Institute for Community Organization in 1976, as they expanded their work to other parts of California. Baumann, who served as the executive director of PICO from 1972 through 2008, had worked with community organizing projects in Chicago in the late 1960s under the supervision of Tom Gaudette. Moving to Oakland, he started working with neighborhood associations and block clubs in an effort to change the environment of the city. He had modest success, but found his organizations were not able to rally enough people to command a seat at the table with the people who had the real power to make significant change. And as the 1970s progressed, poor neighborhoods deteriorated, making it even harder to organize individuals and families into effective groups. A staff retreat in 1984 made a decision to shift to a congregation-based approach, based in part on the experience of the IAF in Texas (Wood 2002: 291–4).

Spurred by its success in Oakland with its group Oakland Community Organizations, in the late 1980s PICO helped other California organizations transition to the congregation-based approach. As it expanded from the West Coast to the East and Midwest, PICO characterized its acronym as People Improving Communities through Organizing. PICO doubled in size between 1997 and 2007 to 53 federations in 16 states, employing 150 professional organizers (Whitman 2009: 22). In 2005 it renamed itself PICO National Network, emphasizing the autonomy of its affiliated organizations, and its role providing training and consultation and developing national strategy.

Statewide Action

As its affiliates multiplied and matured, PICO began implementing a strategy of consolidating power in metropolitan areas and starting statewide efforts to influence public policy. PICO California was established in 1994 to test whether local organizations could aggregate their influence in a permanent state power base. PICO leaders were also concerned to see whether state and national activity would strengthen or weaken local work, and to learn how much effort it would take to win at the state or national level. With 19 affiliates in California, PICO had the best opportunity since the IAF in Texas to explore the viability of such work.

PICO began an initiative on children's health, building on the experience of its San José affiliate People Acting in Community Together, which joined with the labor-based Working Partnerships USA in 2000 to create in California the country's first program to cover all children. The Santa Clara County Children's Health Initiative became a model for health insurance programs covering children (Whitman 2009). In Sacramento in 2005 PICO brought together 4,500 leaders from affiliate groups across California to hold a "town hall meeting" with state legislators.

National Action

In 2002 PICO began discussing how it might use its multi-state network to have an impact on national policy. It formulated a national strategy in 2004, a decade after starting work on its state strategy in California, recognizing that federal policies have real and substantial impacts on the local level. Local work was begun with affiliates getting to know their Congressional representatives. Traditionally, local organizations would develop relationships with local elected officials – mayors, city council members, county supervisors, city managers, and school superintendents. Taking up state policy concerns meant adding relationships with state legislators and executive officials. Now PICO affiliates would lobby their Congressional representatives when they were back in their district offices and, on occasion, in Washington, DC (Whitman 2006–7). PICO also began efforts after 2004 to mobilize its affiliates around the country to lobby Congress on such national issues as health care policy, immigration reform, improving public schools, affordable home ownership, prisons and violence, and the federal response to rebuilding New Orleans and the Gulf Coast after Hurricanes Katrina and Rita. In 2013 PICO had 55 local and regional affiliates in 18 states, Central America, and Rwanda.

The Gamaliel Foundation

The Gamaliel Foundation has focused on projects that would provide greater regional equity in major metropolitan areas, including a special emphasis on transportation equity. The Gamaliel Foundation was created in Chicago in 1968 to assist the Contract Buyers League, which was helping to protect homeowners forced to buy houses on contract. Low-income African Americans could not obtain conventional mortgages, giving them no alternative to buying on contract – which often contained unfair terms that put their home ownership in danger. Gamaliel was reoriented to focus on community organizing when Gregory Galluzzo was hired as executive director in 1986. Seeing its basic function as training and leadership development, Gamaliel's stated goal is "to assist local community leaders to create, maintain and expand independent, grassroots, and powerful faith-based community organizations."

Galluzzo, who was born in Portland, Oregon, joined a Jesuit seminary in Mobile, Alabama, at age 18, studying there from 1964 to 1967. He became involved with the civil rights movement of that time and went to Zambia for three years, returning to the West Coast of the United States in 1970. After studying in Cuernavaca with Ivan Illich, Galluzzo moved to Chicago to learn community organizing, planning to return to Africa. In 1971 he began working with the Pilsen Neighbors Community Council (PNCC) and stayed for four years, mentored by Tom Gaudette and Shel Trapp, and rooming with John Baumann, later the founder of PICO (Rathke 2011b). While working at PNCC, Galluzzo met Mary Gonzales, a notable exception to the typical white, male, college-educated organizer of that time. A Mexican American mother of four, Gonzales would come to be considered one of the best organizers and trainers in Chicago (Cruz 1990). Working together, Galluzzo and Gonzales reoriented PNCC from providing social services to advocacy for the community. Finishing his theological studies, Galluzzo returned to the Pacific Northwest in 1975, where he organized community groups in Seattle, Everett,

Tacoma, and Bellingham (interview with author, November 1996). After four years he left the priesthood, returned to Chicago in 1979, and married Mary Gonzales.

Regional Equity

As Gamaliel picked up affiliates in the Midwest in the 1980s (the period when the IAF was headquartered in New York), Galluzzo and Gonzales urged their groups to consolidate into metropolitan organizations. Gamaliel began in earnest to refocus its efforts from neighborhoods to wider metropolitan areas in the early 1990s. ISAIAH, then its affiliate in St. Paul, had been influenced by Myron Orfield, a Minnesota state representative who linked the economic decline of the Twin Cities to the growth of the outer suburbs. Orfield advocated programs of tax sharing to promote regional equity and smart growth. Convinced by Orfield's regional equity analysis of urban sprawl leading to concentrated poverty, ISAIAH found a winnable issue in cleaning up contaminated "brownfield" sites in the Twin Cities.

Orfield spoke to a meeting of Gamaliel's senior staff in December 1995, and the organization soon adopted regional equity organizing as a guiding perspective for the network. Gamaliel established a "strategic partnership" with Orfield, former Albuquerque mayor David Rusk, and john powell, then director of the University of Minnesota's Institute on Race and Poverty. These policy experts served as consultants on metropolitan organizing strategies and speakers at meetings and conferences (Galluzzo 2009; Kleidman 2004: 408–9).

Gamaliel and Barack Obama

Gamaliel began to receive widespread public attention only with the 2008 Presidential campaign of Barack Obama. While liberals were generally pleased to learn that Obama had worked as a community organizer before he entered law school, conservatives quickly began looking for activity that would portray him as a radical hostile to American ideals and basic principles. While working as an organizer and a trainer for Gamaliel's Developing Communities Project, Obama was mentored by Greg Galluzzo, Jerry Kellman, and Mike Kruglik (who later left Gamaliel to found the organization Building One America to promote the regional equity agenda).

Conservative writer Stanley Kurtz has tried to tie Obama's work in far south Chicago for the Gamaliel affiliate to the controversial Rev. Jeremiah Wright and former Weather Underground leader Bill Ayers. Placing a major focus on Gamaliel's emphasis on regionalism, Kurtz argues that Gamaliel and Obama's intent is to "abolish suburbs" by such devices as forced annexation and tax-base sharing between suburbs and metropolitan centers. What Gamaliel describes positively as regional and tax equity, Kurtz sees negatively as redistribution of wealth (Kurtz 2012: 1–47). Kurtz writes that Obama's debt to Alinsky consists chiefly of "pragmatism, stealth, left radicalism, and confrontation" (Kurtz 2012: 88).

Transportation Equity and TEN

The Transportation Equity Network (TEN) is a national coalition of some 350 organizations in 41 states, now operating as a project of the Gamaliel Foundation. TEN was initiated by the Center for Community Change in Washington, DC, in 1997 to fight for a fair share of transportation services for poor communities, and to impact federal transportation policy (Swanstrom and Barrett 2007). In August 2005 TEN achieved a victory with passage of the Safe, Accountable, Flexible, Efficient Transportation Equity Act – A Legacy for Users. The Act included language proposed by TEN that involves local residents in transportation planning and sets aside money for equity research. TEN also pushed for workforce development language in the reauthorization of a federal transportation bill. TEN's current priorities include fair access to transportation-related jobs, increased funding for mass transit, increased community input to local and state planning for transit, and smart and equitable growth.

Tensions

Gamaliel discovered it is no easy matter running a multi-racial, multi-ethnic, and multi-class organization, undergoing rapid expansion, that listens to all voices and provides equal opportunities for all (including women). Discontent from the grassroots bubbled up within Gamaliel in the mid-2000s. The African American Leadership Commission (AALC) registered growing tension with the Gamaliel national leadership, which was largely white and male. The executive committee of the AALC resigned. An "Inclusion & Racial Equity Task Force" was established, and conducted extensive surveys and interviews among the affiliates. The Task Force issued its report in June 2008.

The report, "Faith & Democracy," noted that building multi-racial coalitions for racial justice is difficult work in largely uncharted territory. At the same time, it is essential that groups leading such work address internal race and gender issues in a deliberate fashion. A central tension was the contradiction between top-down vs. bottom-up determination of priorities, with the Gamaliel central staff perceived as committed to creating a national power organization, at the cost of grassroots organizing and empowerment of new and emerging leaders. The centralization of power was seen as disempowering women and people of color. The hierarchy of power gave too much authority to the mostly white male central staff and too little to the affiliates. Job descriptions were undeveloped and accountability was unclear. Greater transparency about funding and the allocation of resources was necessary, as was open communication between affiliates and the central staff (Gamaliel Foundation 2008: 1–8).

An interesting element of the report raised concerns about the Alinsky organizing approach, with its emphasis on a confrontational style and "color-blind" assumptions. The stress on gaining power can privilege those comfortable with a "masculine conflict-oriented style," and disadvantage women and stifle the voices of those comfortable with more nurturing roles (Gamaliel Foundation 2008: 8–11). Partly as a result of the "Faith & Democracy" report, Gamaliel now has perhaps the most extensive structure of participation of any of the large congregation-based networks: a council of affiliate presidents, the African American Leadership Council, a clergy caucus, an annual retreat for women leaders and staff called Ntosake, a Civil Rights of Immigrants Task Force, and an annual conference called the International Leadership Assembly.

Gamaliel also has the first woman of color to head one of the leading congregation-based organizing networks in the Alinsky tradition: Ana Garcia-Ashley. Born in the Dominican Republic and an immigrant to the United States, Garcia-Ashley was hired in 2011 as executive director upon the retirement of founding executive Greg Galluzzo. Since 1992 Garcia-Ashley had been the lead organizer of Gamaliel's Milwaukee affiliate, MICAH, which won a $500 million commitment from local banks to finance affordable housing. She was also the founding head of WISDOM, Gamaliel's statewide network in Wisconsin. As of 2014 Gamaliel had 45 affiliates in 17 states, the United Kingdom, and South Africa.

National People's Action

National People's Action (NPA) was founded in Chicago in 1972 by community activist Gale Cincotta, one of the first women to head a community organizing network, and community organizer Shel Trapp, a former Methodist minister. Cincotta began organizing as a PTA leader on Chicago's West Side, working to get more resources for her six sons' schools. She joined Organization for a Better Austin (OBA) in the mid-1960s, where she met IAF organizer Tom Gaudette and Shel Trapp, who was director of OBA. Cincotta became president of OBA, and began a long-standing partnership with Trapp.

One of the most important problems confronting the Austin area at that time was "red-lining" by banks and insurance companies, which were refusing to lend to new homeowners and businesses in the rapidly changing neighborhoods. Cincotta and Trapp assembled a coalition of neighborhood, church, union, and seniors' groups. As it became clear that action was needed on a national scale, they called a national grassroots housing conference in Chicago in 1972, and formed NPA. They also set up the National Training and Information Center (NTIC), of which Cincotta was the executive director, as their training arm (Westgate 2011).

The subsequent annual meetings of NPA were held in Washington, DC, where participants could lobby for Congressional action. NPA helped write and pass the Home Mortgage Disclosure Act of 1975, the Community Reinvestment Act of 1977, and the National Affordable Housing Act of 1990 (Westgate 2011). To get the laws implemented, Cincotta confronted federal agencies and local lenders with raucous demonstrations and direct action. In 1984 she negotiated an agreement with three Chicago banks to provide $173 million for low-interest loans to poor neighborhoods in the city. A writer for the *Wall Street Journal* called her "the leading advocate of forcing banks to lend to the poor" (Bailey 1985).

NPA survived the retirement of Trapp in 2000 and the death of Cincotta in 2001 with a transition to new leadership cultivated within its ranks. The NTIC, as the "501(c)(3)," or tax-exempt "charitable and educational," organization, had been the primary vehicle for attracting funding from foundations and corporations (some 80 percent of its financial support) as well as federal contracts. Joe Mariano, who worked at the NTIC for 20 years, took over as executive director of the Center after Cincotta's death. With Cincotta and Trapp gone, financial support began to dwindle. A US Department of Justice audit of federal contracts in 2008 showed that some funds from the early 2000s had been used illegally for lobbying. NPA settled for $550,000, and the NTIC executive director accepted a plea bargain and served five months in prison. NPA closed the NTIC, reorganized its network, and began to depend more on support from its member organizations. Presently NPA supports three campaigns from the local to the state and national level: Bank Accountability, Housing Justice, and Immigrant and Workers' Rights.

During 2012, NPA affiliates began an effort to define a long-term agenda for the network, working with Richard Healey's Grassroots Policy Project as a strategic partner. Members were challenged to re-imagine what is possible, to set out a vision of democracy and a new economy that would inspire a movement. NPA's principles of the new economy include democratic control of capital, racial justice, corporations serving the common good, real democracy, and ecological sustainability. Intended as a 40-year program, the agenda is not a blueprint but a guide connecting one campaign to the next. The agenda shifts the focus of NPA to structural reforms that can eventually culminate in a structural transformation resulting in democratic control of government, public control of the economy, structural equity, community control of local resources, and global sustainability (National People's Action n.d. [2013]).

NPA currently represents over 200 organizers and staff in its 26 affiliates in 14 states. George Goehl, who previously worked at the Center for Community Change, has been executive director since 2007. NPA continues to attract hundreds of people to its annual conference in Washington, DC.

From Citizen Action to USAction

Inspired by their experience with the civil rights, women's, New Left, and labor movements, Heather Booth and Steve Max founded the Midwest Academy in Chicago in 1973 and later the associated Citizen Action network. Heather's husband Paul Booth, a one-time leader of Students for a Democratic Society, had been the first chairman of the Campaign Against Pollution, Alinsky's Chicago-based project battling air pollution – initiated after a summer of intense smog in 1969 – that became the prototype for Citizen Action organizations (Horwitt 1989: 531). Citizen Action affiliates included both statewide membership organizations with local chapters and statewide coalitions of labor, citizen, farm, and senior organizations. Citizen Action pioneered the door-to-door canvass model to recruit members and raise money. It also did extensive electoral work in support of Democratic candidates, and made national health insurance a priority campaign.

In 1997 the national office of Citizen Action was caught up in a scheme to illegally channel money to the reelection campaign of Teamster reform president Ron Carey. Michael Ansara, a Massachusetts telemarketer and long-time activist on the left, admitted laundering money and pleaded guilty to conspiracy charges. Angry affiliates demanded the national office be dissolved.

In 1999 Heather Booth and William McNary, formerly the co-director of Citizen Action Illinois, founded USAction to coordinate the remaining Citizen Action state chapters and help rebuild the network. As of April 2014, USAction claimed 25 affiliates in 22 states, including associated national union allies the Service Employees International Union, the American Federation of State County and Municipal Employees, and the Communication Workers of America. McNary served as USAction's president from 1999 to 2012. The executive director is Fred Azcarte, who formerly led Jobs with Justice for 15 years, then directed the Voice@Work Campaign of the AFL-CIO.

ACORN

An important difference among community organizations is "individual members vs. organizational members," sometimes described as "neighborhood organizing vs. institutional organizing." Alinsky thought it required less time, effort, and money to "organize the organized" than to "organize the unorganized." ACORN was the leading association of individual member groups, until internal scandal and external attack brought the organization to bankruptcy and collapse in 2011. As many observers saw ACORN as the most successful and most promising of the organizing vehicles (see Fisher 2009), it is important to understand the sources of its vulnerability and learn what lessons can be drawn from its experience.

ACORN, the Association of Community Organizations for Reform Now, began in 1970 as a spin-off from the National Welfare Rights Organization, founded by George Wiley, who enlisted civil rights workers and trained them in an Alinsky-influenced program at Syracuse University (Kotz and Kotz 1977). From a base in Arkansas, Wade Rathke and Gary Delgado developed a replicable approach to forming individual membership organizations and developing leaders in low-income neighborhoods – mostly black and Hispanic – relying substantially on young, mostly white, middle-class staff working for subsistence wages (Atlas 2010). The Institute for Social Justice served as ACORN's training arm. Although ACORN got its start in a predominantly rural state, most of its branches were in urban and inner-city areas. In a candid admission, Rathke acknowledged that with rural populations thinned by outmigration, "we never could figure out how to build something big that members could sustain unless there were enough of them to make it work" (Rathke 2008: 68).

ACORN established local housing corporations to rehabilitate homes and provide home ownership counseling services. It successfully pressured banks to provide mortgages and home improvement loans in low-income communities (Delgado 1986). ACORN departed in a number of significant ways from the Alinsky tradition model, particularly as developed by the "modern IAF." ACORN recruited individual members by going door-to-door in their target neighborhoods. (But recall that Fred Ross did the same in building the CSO in California, with the help of Cesar Chavez, while both worked for the IAF.) ACORN was not structured as a federation of local and state groups, but was a single national organization, run from a central headquarters. This gave it the ability to conduct highly coordinated national campaigns, but had the downside of a long-term national leadership that grew administratively careless (Rathke served as chief organizer for nearly 40 years, from 1970 to 2008) and left the entire organization vulnerable to scandal. Most of the long-term leaders were white males, a fact that rankled organizers of color, many of whom were women, although their numbers reached a majority of the organizer staff by the early 2000s.

In 1976 Rathke drew up his "20/80 plan" for ACORN to expand from three states to 20 by 1980, mostly starting from scratch (in addition to Arkansas, ACORN had a foothold in the Dallas-Fort Worth area in Texas, and in Sioux Falls, South Dakota). In a few cases ACORN affiliated existing groups, such as California's Citizens Action League (Atlas 2010: 39–42; Kotz and

Kotz 1977: 204). With organizations in 20 states, ACORN would have a base to elect independent delegates to the Democratic Party convention in sufficient numbers to influence platform policy on issues important to low- and moderate-income people.

ACORN's involvement with politics, particularly its outside/ inside relationship to the Democratic Party, was another departure from the norms of the Alinsky tradition of organizing. ACORN jumped into electoral politics, running candidates for non-partisan offices and helping form two minor parties, the New Party and the more successful (in New York state) Working Families Party. ACORN took leadership of Project Vote in 2003, and registered nearly a million voters (mostly low-income and people of color) for the 2008 Presidential election.

On housing issues, ACORN joined the loose coalition led by NPA to end red-lining and other discrimination by banks and savings and loan companies. Passage of the Home Mortgage Disclosure Act in 1975 and the Community Reinvestment Act in 1977 were important victories. ACORN formed its own Housing Corporation to considerable success, but it left ACORN highly dependent on federal government funding – another situation Alinsky had advised community organizations to avoid. Another successful ACORN program that promoted use of the Earned Income Tax Credit by low-income working people was also sup- ported by federal government money.

Unlike most congregation-based networks, ACORN forged long-term alliances with labor unions, and in fact started its own United Labor Union to organize fast-food workers. ACORN led "living wage" campaigns in many cities, after the IAF had proven unable to motivate its affiliates to replicate its first success with a living wage ordinance in Baltimore.

Expanding rapidly in the 1980s and 1990s, ACORN claimed some 350,000 member families in 850 neighborhood chapters in over 100 cities in 38 states, before a series of crises brought the organization down. The first was a $2 million embezzlement by Dale Rathke, the younger brother of founder Wade Rathke. Discovered in 2000, the financial loss had been kept secret for eight years from ACORN's board of directors. The theft and cover-up was made possible by a lack of adequate financial controls over the complicated maze of some 200 corporations set up by ACORN to run business operations in various states. The board of directors was outraged. Dale Rathke was fired, and Wade Rathke was forced to resign after 38 years directing the organization. Bertha Lewis was hired to take his place. The Catholic Campaign for Human Development, under pressure from conservatives in the church, ended its funding. Foundations cut off support (Atlas 2010: 221–5).

The second scandal, in 2009, was a trumped-up set of staged interviews, recorded with a concealed video camera, with local ACORN office staff by conservative activists Hannah Giles and James O'Keefe, posing as a prostitute and her pimp. (A San Diego employee fired by ACORN when the videos were released later recovered substantial financial settlements from Giles and O'Keefe.) Together the scandals frightened off funders, prompting conservatives in Congress to cut off funds to ACORN, and the organization went bankrupt. A few state affiliates incorporated under new names. ACORN's California operation has become the Alliance of Californians for Community Empowerment (ACCE), and the New York branch is now New York Communities for Change. Madeline Talbott had earlier taken ACORN's Chicago operation independent as Action Now (Schutz and Sandy 2011: 114–52).

Wade Rathke continues as the chief organizer of ACORN International, which has affiliates in Canada, Argentina, Mexico, Peru, the Dominican Republic, Honduras, India, Kenya, South Korea, the Czech Republic, and Italy. He is a founder and board member of the Organizer's Forum. He is also publisher and editor-in-chief of *Social Policy*, the quarterly journal covering organizing, a publication of the nonprofit Labor Neighbor Research and Training Center.

Generational Shift

A major generational shift is occurring in the leading networks in the Alinsky tradition. Replacing a leader is often an unsettling process, particularly when the leader is a founder who has served as chief executive for many years. There's a name for it: founder's syndrome. Charismatic founders can have trouble deciding when to step down. Not only can they find it difficult to retire, but procedures for choosing successors may not be in place. Boards of directors may be figureheads accustomed to ratifying the leader's decisions, not determining the organization's direction under changing circumstances (S.M. Miller 2012).

As noted above, PICO's founder John Baumann retired at the end of 2008. In a selection that signaled continuity, Scott Reed, on the PICO staff for 30 years, was named executive director. Ed Chambers retired in 2009, but evidently the IAF can't decide in which direction it wants to move. An interim arrangement has four senior organizers rotating the executive responsibilities. The Gamaliel Foundation's Greg Galluzzo retired at the end of 2010, and was succeeded in January 2011, as we saw, by Ana Garcia-Ashley. The appointment of Garcia-Ashley, a bilingual Afro-Caribbean woman born in the Dominican Republic, was controversial within Gamaliel and prompted a couple of passed-over senior staff to leave the organization. Garcia-Ashley has moved to develop new relationships and alliances with other advocacy organizations, including unions, civil rights groups, and environmentalists. Also as noted, NPA organizer Shel Trapp retired in 2000 and leader Gale Cincotta died the following year; George Goehl has been NPA executive director since 2007.

The consequences of the younger generation taking over would appear to include a willingness to cooperate with other networks, unions, and such SMOs as the NAACP. Younger organizers have less of a stake in the quarrels of the network founders. Of the CBCOs, Gamaliel is the most likely to embrace secular groups, both as members of affiliates and as coalition allies. The IAF has a reputation for being the least interested in working with other organizations. In a 1996 interview with Ed Chambers of the IAF, I asked him whether he could imagine cooperation with the other congregation-based community organizing networks. His reply: "The Protestants have 500 denominations. The Catholic Church has divisions. The Jewish faith has its divisions. Why should anyone expect us secular organizers to unite?" The answer, of course, is that the community organizing networks are, or ought to be, pursuing the common good. Although PICO seeks to limit its affiliates to congregation-based groups, it is willing to work in coalitions at the state and national policy levels.

Funding Community Organizing

Ideally, community organizations would maximize their independence by raising all their money from member dues and local fundraising activities. In reality, foundation support has remained a necessity for most of the community-based groups and for the networks' central offices. The major liberal foundations – Ford, Rockefeller, Carnegie – have taken various initiatives to support community organizing. Protestant Church national bodies have been important financial supporters. At the local level, family and community foundations have often played an important role. But the steady mainstay for funding congregation-based and broad-based community organizations over the last 45 years has been the Catholic Campaign for Human Development.

The Catholic Campaign for Human Development

Initiated by a resolution of the United States Catholic Conference (USCC) in 1969, the Campaign for Human Development (CHD) was intended as a response to "the problems of poverty, racism, and social tensions." (The USCC merged with the National Conference of Catholic Bishops in 2001 to form the United States Conference of Catholic Bishops, the organization that now sponsors the CCHD. As we will see below, the CHD added "Catholic" to its name in 1998, hence becoming the CCHD.) Financed by an annual collection during the Thanksgiving season in Catholic parishes across the country, the CHD raised over $250 million in its first 25 years from 1970 to 1995 (Campaign for Human Development 1995: 2). In the 18 years from 1981 to 1999, nearly

$28 million was given in 755 grants to members of the four major faith-based networks: the IAF, PICO, Gamaliel, and DART (Wood 2002: 292).

The degree of Catholic Church support for community organizing is not difficult to understand. Although Alinsky was a secular Jew, he carefully cultivated the Catholic hierarchy of Chicago. The leaders of the principal congregation-based networks are predominantly Roman Catholic. Ed Chambers of the IAF was a seminarian. Of the current quadrumvirate running the IAF, at least one – Sr. Christine Stephens – is a Catholic. In addition, as was noted above, John Baumann, the former leader of PICO, is a Jesuit priest, as was Greg Galluzzo, long-time director of the Gamaliel Foundation. Galluzzo's successor, Ana Garcia-Ashley, is a practicing Catholic. Social movements that appear to be headed for success can inspire counter-movements, and it is not surprising that the support given community organizing by the Catholic Church has provoked a counter-movement by conservative Catholics to defund the faith-based as well as the secular networks.

Conservative Critics

From 1959 to 1964 the Chicago-based, Protestant-oriented magazine *The Christian Century* attacked Alinsky variously as a Marxist fomenting class warfare and a tool of the Catholic Church's attempt to take over Chicago (Finks 1984: 141–4). Rael and Erich Isaac (1985) took the CHD to task for funding radical causes. In the early 1990s a conservative Catholic group, the Wanderer Forum Foundation (now known as the Bellarmine Forum), began to criticize the CHD's relationship with the IAF, and commissioned a commentary with extensive background material on the CHD that was distributed widely within the Catholic Church in 1997. A second commentary was sent to all US Catholic bishops the following year. Responding to the criticism, the bishops added the word "Catholic" to the title of the organization (now the CCHD), and tightened up guidelines to require that funded organizations not endorse policies that are contrary to Catholic doctrine.

Stephanie Block, the author of the commentaries, has recently published a four-volume series titled *Change Agents: Alinskyian Organizing among Religious Bodies* (Block 2012a, 2012b, 2012c, 2012d). In Volume 4 (Block 2012d: 109–75), she summarizes the conservative case against "Alinskyian community organizing," as she calls it, especially regarding the participation of religious institutions in the congregation-based networks:

- The methods of house meetings, small groups, and other training build an illusion of consensus that leaves many congregation members behind as organizers proceed with their programs.
- Ethical questions abound; networks misrepresent their base by claiming the support of every person in every member organization.
- Organizers teach that the end justifies the means.
- Real leadership of the networks comes from the top, not the grassroots; executive staff and organizers have the power to determine long-range strategy. The idea that Alinskyian organizations represent "the people" is thus an illusion.
- The Alinskyian notions that differences are invariably antagonistic and opponents are "enemies" are uncharitable.
- The networks support health care reform without regard to the provision of birth control and abortion services in the plans, contrary to Catholic doctrine.
- Alinskyian organizing presents itself as non-partisan, but in reality it tilts strongly toward progressive politics.
- Alinskyians borrow selectively from the religious traditions and documents of a church, subverting and distorting its true religious meaning.

"Alinskyian organizing networks," Block concludes, "do not serve the poor, do not promote democracy, and do not foster social justice" (Block 2012d: 175).

There is enough "half-truth" to the slanted interpretations in these charges to give them a surface plausibility to the reader unfamiliar with the reality of community organizing. In any case, they have more credibility than the conspiracy theories of the far right. The conservative polemics against the Alinsky tradition are beginning to have an effect. By 2012 several Catholic bishops in the United States refused to sign off on CCHD grants to previously funded local organizations – in effect, vetoing the grants – sometimes based only upon the local group's membership in one of the national networks. The installation of Pope Francis in 2013, with his emphasis on the poor and his background as a Franciscan, could, however, serve to offset the influence of conservative Catholics, and build support for community organizing.

Although a decline in financial resources supplied to community organizations by the Catholic Church may slow the development of new groups, the concepts and tools of the Alinsky tradition are so well known and widely disseminated that they will live on with or without a steady supply of CCHD funding. Nevertheless, the situation emphasizes the need for community organizations to rely more on internally generated funds and less on grant sources.

The newer networks have been important sources of innovation for the practice of community organizing, going beyond the neighborhood and city to metropolitan, regional, state, and national policy issues. While the IAF has kept to the methodologies formulated and refined by its senior organizers Chambers, Cortes, Gecan, and Graf, other networks have been able, by choice or necessity, to explore a variety of approaches that still remain within the spirit of the Alinsky tradition. Pushing at the edges of community organizing are new approaches to electoral politics, some of which draw on techniques from the Alinsky tradition and others that are based in new technologies. We look at some important examples of these in the next chapter.

6

Organizing and Electoral Politics

The Alinsky tradition of community organizing has provided a baseline of perspectives and practices that have long been used by organizers in other contexts, including union organizing, grassroots advocacy organizations, SMOs, and political campaigns. The field of organizing is not a static body of knowledge; new understandings of leadership, motivation, and strategy are being incorporated into organizers' practice. Communication technology has added tools that are being integrated into organizing. Essential knowledge from community organizing has been adapted, modified, and applied to electoral campaigns and social movements. The ideas of Marshall Ganz in particular have been used by the Obama campaign, MoveOn.org, and other groups seeking to activate a grassroots base around elections. Ganz's writing and teaching about the sources of strategic capacity in organizations, the power of story in organizing, and the nature of leadership in organizations and movements have had considerable influence on a new generation of organizers.

Marshall Ganz

Ganz had completed his junior year at Harvard when he went south to participate in the 1964 Mississippi Summer Project. He dropped out of Harvard to work for the United Farm Workers (UFW) in California for 16 years, after which he worked as a trainer and organizer for political campaigns, unions, and nonprofit groups. He returned to Harvard in 1991 to finish his bachelor's degree and stayed on to earn a Ph.D. in sociology in 2000. He is presently a senior lecturer at the Kennedy School of Government at Harvard University.

Strategic Capacity

Ganz's 2009 book *Why David Sometimes Wins* tells the story of his time working with Cesar Chavez and the UFW. He is interested in how Chavez and the UFW succeeded in organizing farm workers when earlier attempts by leftists and well-financed recent efforts by AFL-CIO unions and Teamsters had failed. His answer is the UFW's greater strategic capacity. Ganz defines strategy as "how we turn what we have into what we need to get what we want" (Ganz 2009: 8). Three critical elements of strategy are "targeting, tactics, and timing." Targeting involves focusing available resources on likely outcomes. Tactics that make the most of an organization's resources are obviously preferred. Timing acknowledges that there are windows of opportunity that offer greater prospects for success.

Strategic capacity, Ganz argues, consists of three elements: motivation, access to relevant knowledge, and deliberations that lead to new learning. Motivation "enhances creativity by inspiring concentration, enthusiasm, risk taking, persistence, and learning" (Ganz 2009: 12). Relevant knowledge consists of both skills and information, particularly of the domains in which the organization works. Open deliberation is important when facing new problems that require novel solutions. A leadership team's strategic capacity is thus dependent on both biographical and organizational sources: individual diversity in cultural backgrounds and experience, and organizational commitment to internal structures of "legitimacy, power, and deliberation." How an organization handles conflict among its leadership, whether it depends largely on internally generated financial resources, whether leadership is accountable to the constituencies they represent – all influence strategic capacity.

A deeply motivated leadership team with a variety of experiences and viewpoints, and a deliberative process open to innovation, greatly enhances an organization's strategic capacity (Ganz 2009: 10–19). Broad-based community organizing truly deserving of that title – including unions, environmental organizations, and advocacy groups as well as religious congregations – should be well positioned to take advantage of its diversity to develop innovative tactics and strategies to accomplish its goals.

Public Narrative

Ganz's father was a rabbi and his mother a teacher. After the Second World War, his father was an army chaplain in Germany for three years. The experience of working with Holocaust survivors led his father to impress upon Marshall the perils of anti-Semitism and racism. Recognizing the religious and ethical sources of his motivation to be an organizer, Ganz emphasizes the importance of values in organizing.

Ganz recalls Rabbi Hillel's famous three questions: "If I am not for myself, who will be? If I am for myself alone, what am I? If not now, when?" From these questions, Ganz derives the story of self, the story of us, and the story of now. In his paper "What is Public Narrative?" (Ganz 2008) he writes:

> A story of self communicates who I am – my values, my experience, why I do what I do. A story of us communicates who we are – our shared values, our shared experience, and why we do what we do. And a story of now transforms the present into a moment of challenge, hope, and choice.

Telling the story of self, in Ganz's view, is a key to conducting successful one-on-one conversations, and thus the basis of solid public relationships between people. The ability to tell the story (or "narrative") of self is vital to exercising leadership, and the ability to train or teach the telling of the story of self is a core competency for leaders (Ganz 2010).

Public narrative is the art of translating values into action through stories. Stories are important in organizing because they allow us to express our values not as abstract principles, but as lived experiences, which are able to inspire others. Similarly, organizations must develop a public narrative that captures their goals and mission in compelling terms. Stories help catalyze action by drawing out motivation that results in a commitment to act. Stories are crafted of three elements: character, plot, and moral. Key components of a plot include challenge, choice, and outcome. The character faces an unexpected challenge, has to make a choice, which leads to an outcome from which we draw the moral, or point of the story. We thus construct our story of self around choice points that illuminate our values (Ganz 2008).

In his paper on "The Power of Story in Social Movements," Ganz (2001) summarized his view of how story is related to agency, identity, and strategy: "Social movements tell a new story. In this way they acquire leadership, gain adherents, and develop a capability of mobilizing needed resources to achieve success. Social movements are not merely reconfigured networks and redeployed resources. They are new stories of whom their participants hope to become."

Leadership

A third theme of Ganz's writing and teaching has been leadership, which he defines as "accepting responsibility to create conditions that enable others to achieve shared purpose in the face of uncertainty" (Ganz 2010: 509). "Leaders," in Ganz's terminology, can refer to either staff organizers or volunteer leaders. Ganz identifies five practices that he sees as vital to leadership in social movements: relationships, stories, strategy, action, and structure.

Relationships begin with an exchange of interests and resources, and move to being a true relationship when there is a mutual commitment to a shared future. In the structured context of building an organization, one-on-ones may be used to initiate contacts that may develop into public relationships.

The craft of learning to tell the *stories* of one's self and of the organization is an essential leadership skill. The public narrative, as described in the previous section, reveals values and emotions, and leads to action. Borrowing from psychologist Jerome Bruner, Ganz notes that we map the world both cognitively (analysis) and affectively (emotion). When we find a great discrepancy between "the world as it is" and "the world as it should be," we may be inspired to act to reduce the difference. Regarding action, analysis can answer the "how" question, but only emotion can answer the "why" question – engaging our values and motivation. But the prospect of action can be frightening; here leaders can bring hope, helping people gain confidence with small victories, and finding solidarity with fellow movement members.

Strategy, for Ganz, is using the human and financial resources we have in an effective way to attain our objective (Ganz 2010: 530). As the movement's financial resources are most likely far less than its opponent's, movement organizations may be challenged to focus a commitment on a single strategic outcome for a sustained period.

Action, to Ganz, is "the work of mobilizing and deploying resources to achieve outcomes." Social movements are about "changing the world, not yearning for it, thinking about it, or exhorting it" (Ganz 2010: 535). Resources obtained from outside the organization – say, from foundations – leave participants accountable to the donors. Resources from participants tend to focus on those results desired by the participants. Action also raises the question of allies and collaborators. The greatest challenge for action is getting specific commitments from participants for "time, money, or action." Effective action also depends on having measurable outcomes with deadlines. Part of an organizer's job can be seen as coaching volunteer leaders in taking effective action. Forming leadership teams that draw on participants' varied skills is important both with core teams in member organizations and with the leadership council representing member groups of an institution-based community organization.

Structure is essential to equipping organizations to engage in successful action for change. Managing time is important. Although work toward the organization's goals goes on all year, quarters of the year can be planned to emphasize fundraising in one quarter, issue assemblies in another, public meetings for accountability in a third, and issue task force work in a fourth. Seasonal celebrations can build confidence, optimism, and solidarity as well as raise money for the organization.

In a pilot project with the Sierra Club, Ganz and his Harvard psychology colleague Ruth Wageman (Ganz and Wageman 2010) addressed three structural challenges: "the organization of leadership," "effective deliberation and decision making," and "mechanisms of accountability." Steering away from the model of the heroic individual, they built leadership teams, taught collaborative skills in the context of their use, and embedded accountability into the team process. Similar leadership development could be a substantial benefit to groups with a grassroots base seeking to ally themselves with IBCOs (Ganz 2010: 542–3). Nevertheless, it is clear from the Sierra Club experiment that a commitment from the top leadership is essential to transform the organizational culture at the local chapter level. Without strong support from the executive director and board leadership, a few local groups may develop an organizing culture, but most will continue as a collection of individuals, not as an organizing team.

OFA

Ganz helped design the training for the 2008 Presidential primary and general election campaign organization Obama for America, through a two-day training experience called "Camp Obama." After the 2008 election, the campaign changed its name to Organizing for America, became part of the Democratic National Committee in 2009, and continued for a time to train new volunteers through "Camp OFA." Following the 2012 Presidential election, the group changed its name again to Organizing for Action, becoming an independent 501(c)(4) organization in 2013 (contributions to which are not tax deductible as they are in the case of charities).

In this latest iteration, OFA is "a grassroots organization dedicated to supporting the agenda Americans voted for on November 8, 2012." In other words, OFA is committed to issue organizing,

119

not electoral campaigning. In practical terms, this means supporting the legislative agenda of President Obama. OFA will train and
develop grassroots leaders, build coalition partnerships in states
and nationally, develop state organizations that fundraise at the
grassroots to become self-sustaining, and get its story into the
media.

OFA's priority issue campaigns as of early 2014 were:

- gun violence prevention;
- comprehensive immigration reform;
- climate change;
- the Affordable Care Act;
- stand with women.

OFA's national strategy is to win issue victories through local
initiatives. OFA has over 200 chapters nationwide, at various
stages of development, with offices in every state. The national
and state structures have paid staff, while local chapters have an
overall volunteer lead, issue team and neighborhood leads, and
general volunteers. Chapters are organized around Congressional
Districts and major media markets. Early in 2014 OFA announced
a training program for some 1,570 organizing fellows to prepare
for the 2014 and 2016 elections and beyond.

Camp Obama Training

The initial Obama for America training for the fall 2008 campaign took place at several Camp Obama locations. Ganz's
ideas were evident in the basic orientation to OFA. Volunteers
were introduced to the "story of self" and the "story of us,"
and practiced telling their story of self in two minutes or less.
Volunteer recruitment for local work emphasized building relationships rooted in shared values and confirmed by commitment.
The classic "one-on-one" meeting was taught as a key tool to
developing relationships. As developed in community organizing, one-on-ones were to be scheduled, purposeful, intentional,
and probing. The remainder of the training dealt with Obama

campaign issues, phone banking, neighborhood team development, and getting out the vote on election day. Californians were also briefed on working out of state in Nevada and New Mexico (Obama for America 2008).

Following Obama's 2008 election victory, OFA was working to maintain the volunteer campaign organization it had constructed to help push the President's agenda through Congress. In spring of 2009 new rounds of Camp Obama two-day trainings were conducted around the country. The training maintained the spirit of Ganz's ideas on motivating and developing volunteers into grassroots leaders by treating them according to the principles of "respect, empower, include," the mantra from the fall campaign (Organizing for America 2009). The priority issues were to be energy, health care, and education, but the major emphasis shifted quickly to Obama's health care proposal. Together with MoveOn and Health Care for America Now, OFA pushed for a "public option" in the Affordable Care Act, but fell two votes short in the Senate.

MoveOn

MoveOn.org (MoveOn for short) was founded in 1988 by Joan Blades and Wes Boyd, internet entrepreneurs whose software company was famous for its "flying toasters" screen saver. Fed up with the politics of the scandal involving President Bill Clinton and White House intern Monica Lewinsky, Blades and Boyd set up a website with a petition asking Congress to censure President Clinton and move on. They got 100,000 signatures the first week, and figured they were on to something. As MoveOn developed, it kept its core staff small, numbering 20 to 30 in the 2008 to 2012 period. There is no MoveOn central office and there are no field offices, and key staff are scattered across the country. Contact and consultation are maintained through email, chat, cell phones, and conference calls (Karpf 2012: 27–31).

MoveOn has a rather expansive definition of membership, which includes anyone who gives money to the organization, signs a petition, or signs up to attend a local event and gives a valid email address. With this definition, MoveOn counted around 8 million members as of 2014.

Local MoveOn activists began meeting in substantial numbers in demonstrations opposing the Iraq war. Some MoveOn leaders thought the combination of online activism plus the face-to-face interaction at the local level could be a powerful combination. After Obama's election in 2008, in early 2009 MoveOn hired 11 full-time field organizers (some of whom had worked in the Obama campaign) to support the council network. Each council had a volunteer council coordinator (later organizer, or CO), and each four or five councils had a volunteer regional organizer (RO). The staff field organizer had a weekly conference call with all the volunteer COs and ROs. Some 150 viable councils existed by 2012, with a membership approaching 20,000 volunteers. With core teams ranging from five to 20 people, perhaps 2,000 activists made work with MoveOn a real priority.

Training in "Camp MoveOn" and After

To train the COs and ROs, MoveOn turned to Marshall Ganz for an organizing model for its "Camp MoveOn." An early version was held in Colorado in 2009, and a larger National Leadership Training was held in Washington, DC, in March 2010. Some regional Camp MoveOn trainings were also held later that year, and a conference-call version with six weekly installments, called the Council Organizing Academy, was conducted on a national basis in fall 2011 and spring 2012. Basic organizing tools were covered: telling the story of self, conducting one-on-one interviews, defining specific and winnable objectives for campaigns. Some materials on the cycle of building the base, building councils, building leaders, and building campaigns were borrowed from the School of Unity and Liberation (SOUL), a center for training grassroots organizers in Oakland, California.

With the emergence of the Occupy movement in the fall of 2011, the dynamics of local organizing began to shift a bit for

MoveOn, and the national organization joined the coalition that was planning "The 99% Spring" training for April 2012. The training covered three components: the economic crisis, the history of nonviolent social movements in the United States, and practicing nonviolent direct action tactics. For a program put together by a committee, the training was reasonably coherent, but lacked a sense of context. Nonviolent direct action was not presented as one tactic in MoveOn's repertoire (also including lobbying, petitions, boycotts, elections, etc.), but as the all-purpose tactic.

The question may be moot. After Obama was reelected in November 2012, MoveOn experienced a falling off of financial contributions. Forced to rethink its program, it decided to let its grassroots members initiate petition campaigns on whatever local, state, or national issues they wished. The "Million Leaders" project builds on the successful response to the SignOn.org site launched by MoveOn in 2012 (Weiner 2013). The paid field organizer staff positions were eliminated, and MoveOn's local councils were on their own. The volunteer COs and ROs held together through 2013 in such states as California, New York, and Massachusetts, but when MoveOn's national leadership said they would circulate all petitions, whether progressive or conservative, a majority of the remaining volunteer organizers protested. The viability of MoveOn's local council structure is in doubt as of early 2014.

MoveOn was the first wildly successful venture in mobilizing activists through online communications. Its even greater promise was combining online activity with face-to-face local councils – one, however, to which the organization's board and staff were never fully committed. Having no democratic mechanisms for the grassroots to give feedback to the MoveOn board and staff leadership, the organization burned through its local volunteer leadership as if there were an infinite supply of people who would follow whatever direction the staff set for the moment (see Walls 2012). Nevertheless, MoveOn undeniably changed the under-standing of the contribution to be made by mass email. Although community organizing is only beginning to explore how to make effective use of internet resources, it will be different after the "MoveOn effect" (Weiner 2013). We can expect community organizing networks to make extensive use of websites, social media, Twitter, email petitions, conference calls, webinars, and no doubt programs yet to be devised.

7

Alternative Approaches

Although the Alinsky tradition may be dominant, there are other approaches to community organizing that merit attention. Excluding those activities that are more appropriately classified as community development, this chapter will address three alternative varieties of community organizing.

The first is a critical practice from the left, generally known as popular education. The Highlander Research and Education Center in New Market, Tennessee, is the best-known example. The oldest sponsor of popular education associated with social movements in the United States, Highlander celebrated its 80th anniversary in 2012. Highlander is most closely identified with founder Myles Horton. Organizational consultant Kristina Smock terms this the "transformative model" (Smock 2004: 222–43). Sociologist Aldon Morris puts Highlander in a special class of SMO he calls "movement half-way houses," along with groups like the American Friends Service Committee, the Fellowship of Reconciliation, and the War Resisters League. He defines a movement half-way house as "only partly integrated into the larger society because its participants are actively involved in efforts to bring about a desired change in society" (Morris 1984: 139).

The second alternative is horizontalism, characterized by efforts to reduce hierarchy and flatten the levels of authority within an organization. Horizontalism includes such diverse examples as the anti-nuclear movements, anti-globalization actions and social forums, the Occupy movement, and other projects influenced by feminism or anarchism. Smock (2004) discusses a segment of this approach she calls the "women-centered" model.

The chapter concludes with an outline of the collaborative organizing of John McKnight and John Kretzmann, and Mike Eichler's consensus organizing, which he contrasts to what he calls the conflict organizing of the Alinsky tradition. Smock's "civic model" and her "community-building model" cover the field of collaborative organizing, which she contrasts to the "power-based" Alinsky approach.

Popular Education: The Highlander Center

As an international movement, popular education is best known through the work of Brazilian educator Paulo Freire, author of *Pedagogy of the Oppressed* (1968). In the United States, it is most strongly identified with the work of Myles Horton and the Highlander Research and Education Center (originally known as the Highlander Folk School). Horton grew up in a low-income family in eastern Tennessee, and attended Cumberland University. During the summer before his senior year, he was employed by the Presbyterian Church to conduct vacation Bible school classes in four mountain counties. The experience left him with a conviction that people had solutions to their economic problems if he could only get them together to talk with each other. Graduating in 1928, Horton went to work for the YMCA, visiting high schools and colleges in Tennessee.

Searching for a form of education relevant to the working poor of the Southern mountains, and on the advice of his mentors, Horton enrolled in Union Theological Seminary in New York. There he studied with theologian Reinhold Niebuhr, who became a friend, advisor, and financial supporter of his work. For the academic year 1930–1 Horton went to Chicago to study with noted University of Chicago sociologist Robert E. Park, whose ideas about social conflict and mass movements as vehicles for social change resonated with him. He met a number of times with Jane Addams of Hull House, who encouraged Horton's vision, which sounded to her like a rural version of a settlement house. In fall 1931 Horton traveled to Denmark to visit the folk schools influenced by nineteenth-century Lutheran bishop N.F.S. Grundtvig (Adams 1975: 1–24).

From this blend of Danish folk schools, settlement houses, and social movements, Horton co-founded Highlander Folk School in 1932 with educator Don West and Methodist minister James Dombrowski. They leased a home near Monteagle in Grundy County, Tennessee, from a sympathetic progressive woman. From the 1930s through the mid-1940s Highlander ran educational programs for the labor movement in the South, developing strong relationships with the CIO unions – and generating animosity from the anti-union forces in Southern industries. When the CIO moved to expel Communist-influenced unions in 1949, it ended its educational contracts with Highlander, which refused to cut its ties with those unions alleged to be Communist-dominated. By 1953 the CIO had deserted Highlander, and Horton had shifted his attention to working on the unresolved issues of racial injustice in the South (Glen 1988: 21–46, 70–106).

The shift to working on racial justice in the 1950s and 1960s was well timed to support the emerging civil rights movement. As we noted in Chapter 3, Rosa Parks had attended a 10-day workshop at Highlander headed by Horton a few months before her arrest in December 1955 that launched the Montgomery Bus Boycott. Highlander initiated Citizenship Schools, led by Septima Clark and Bernice Robinson, together with Esau Jenkins and other local people from coastal South Carolina and Georgia, teaching literacy and preparing people from the Sea Islands to register to vote. Highlander also hosted meetings of the newly formed SCLC as well as the young college students who created SNCC.

Such "trouble-making" drew the attention of defenders of the Jim Crow system of segregation. The state of Tennessee revoked the charter of the Highlander Folk School in 1961 and auctioned the property, on the pretext that Highlander was selling beer without a license, had violated its nonprofit charter by giving Horton a house he had built on the school grounds, and taught whites and blacks together in violation of state law (never mind

that this was seven years after *Brown* v. *Board of Education*).
Reincorporated as the Highlander Research and Education Center,
it moved into an old mansion in Knoxville, where it stayed until
1971, when it occupied its present location on a farm near New
Market, Tennessee (Glen 1988: 184–229).

A vital and perhaps unique aspect of Highlander's workshops has
been the music and cultural programs begun by Zilphia Johnson
Horton, who first met Myles when attending a two-month class
at Highlander in 1935. They were married as soon as the class
ended. Zilphia didn't think of music as the entertainment of an
audience by a performer; she saw songs as a medium of participation in which everyone would be singing. After her death from a
tragic accident in 1956, Guy Carawan was recruited to continue
the music program. He took a song Zilphia learned from tobacco
workers attending a Highlander workshop in 1945, kept some
changes made by Pete Seeger, and taught "We Shall Overcome"
to the civil rights movement throughout the South (Horton 1990:
75–8). Guy and his wife Candie Carawan have argued for the
importance of music and culture to social movements, a dimension
that has often been overlooked by community organizers:

> There is a tendency to underestimate the importance of cultural work,
> to feel that music and poetry, dance and humor, will naturally be part
> of community life and attempts to challenge oppression or inequality.
> In our experience, this is not the case. The seeds for cultural expression
> are there, but cultivating and nurturing those seeds are also necessary.
> Not only is it important for individuals to seek out and encourage the
> richness of cultural expression; there also have to be organizations
> and institutions that recognize and support this work. We have been
> fortunate to be a part of one. (Carawan and Carawan 1993: 260)

The rise of the "Black Power" movement in 1965 meant that
Highlander's association with the civil rights movement would
be diminished. Looking for other appropriate fields for action,
it chose to emphasize grassroots organizing in the Appalachian
region. During the Poor People's Campaign in Washington, DC, in
the summer of 1970, Highlander set up camp for a group of mostly
white community people from the mountains; they were one of the

few delegations of whites, if not the only one, who stayed on until the shanty town was torn down. So from the late 1960s through the 1970s and on into the 1980s, Highlander focused on the Southern Appalachians, from West Virginia through the Carolina mountains.

But no unified Appalachian movement developed comparable to the labor movement of the 1930s and 1940s, or to the civil rights movement of the 1950s and 1960s. No charismatic Appalachian leader emerged comparable to John L. Lewis or Martin Luther King, Jr. During the 1990s and 2000s, Highlander expanded its range of activities to include work with recent immigrants, the LGBT community, and environmental justice groups throughout the South. Summarizing Highlander's greatest success, historian John M. Glen wrote, "What Highlander taught above all else was the possibility for blacks and whites to live and work together on an equal basis, something few places in the South could or would permit in the 1950s and early 1960s" (Glen 1988: 172).

What, then, distinguishes popular education from community organizing? In his conversations with Paulo Freire, Horton approaches the question by discussing his relationship with Saul Alinsky. Although both attended the University of Chicago and studied in the sociology department with Professor Robert E. Park in 1931, they did not meet until the 1940s, when Alinsky was organizing in Back of the Yards with the Packinghouse Workers. Horton writes:

> ... that's an old question, it goes way back. Saul Alinsky and I went on a circuit. We had the "Alinsky/Horton show" that went out on the circuit debating and discussing the difference between organizing and education. At that time Saul was a staunch supporter of Highlander, and I was a staunch supporter of him, but we differed and we recognized the difference. ... Saul says that organizing educates. I said that education makes possible organization, but there's a different interest, different emphasis. (Horton and Freire 1990: 115)

Horton believed he and Alinsky disagreed over the importance of winning small victories:

Saul and I differed, because my position was that if I had to make a choice between achieving an objective and utilizing the struggle to develop and radicalize people, my choice would be to let the goal go and develop the people. He believed that organizing success was the way to radicalize people. . . . it's essential to consider whether that organization is moving toward structural reform or limited reform. If it's working toward structural reform, I'll work with that organization. If it's just limited reform, I would hesitate . . . . (Horton 1990: 180)

Mike Miller argues that we shouldn't make organizing and educating into an either–or question. For one reason, a good organizer is also a teacher. Miller quotes a paper, "Making an Offer We Can't Refuse," by IAF organizer Dick Harmon:

Organizing is teaching. Obviously not academic-type teaching, which is confined for the most part to stuffing data into people's ears. Organizing is teaching which rests on people's life experiences, drawing them out, developing trust, going into action, disrupting old perceptions of reality, developing group solidarity, watching the growth of confidence to continue to act, then sharing in the emotional foundation for continual questioning of the then current *status quo* . . . . (Miller 1993: 52)

Anger at injustice is often listed as one of the necessary characteristics that makes a great organizer. Horton understood that persisting in the movement meant adopting the perspective of the long-distance runner. He left this advice on how to stay in the struggle for the long haul by harnessing your anger:

I had to learn that my anger didn't communicate to people what I wanted to communicate. . . . I had to turn my anger into a slow burning fire, instead of a consuming fire. You don't want the fire to go out – you never let it go out – and if it gets weak you stoke it, but you don't want it to burn you up. It keeps you going, but you subdue it, because you don't want to be destroyed by it. . . . I started saying, "Horton, get yourself together, get ready for the long haul and try to determine how you can live out this thing and make your life useful." (Horton 1990: 80–1)

Horton retired as director of Highlander at age 65 in 1970, but kept active on the staff with the residential workshop program until his death at age 84 in 1990. Highlander has had several directors since then; since 1999 all have been women. Pam McMichael has been director since 2005.

So far no one has done for Myles Horton what Ed Chambers did for Saul Alinsky: develop a standardized program that could communicate a replicable approach for doing popular education. Efforts failed in 1969 to create a Highlander West in New Mexico to serve Mexican American and Indian groups, and a similar project for Chicago never got off the ground (Glen 1988: 217). Today there is no standard curriculum or methodology for popular education in the Highlander vein, and there are no replicas of the Highlander Center. However, a strategic assessment and action plan was completed in 2013 by representatives of the Highlander staff, board, and constituency leaders to see what people need in the present context and how Highlander can play its particular role. The plan includes developing a new workshop curriculum on governance and democratic participation in the economy, creation of a new fellowship program on economic transition in Appalachia, increased sharing of its methodologies of popular education and cultural organizing, and expanding its efforts for worker justice (Highlander Research & Education Center 2013).

Horizontalism

The Old Left, with its Marxian certainties – the laws of historical materialism, the crisis of capitalism, the working class as the revolutionary subject, and in its Leninist permutations the vanguard party of the proletariat – seems so twentieth century. Even the wing of the left that never lost sight of democratic ideals – the social democrats and democratic socialists – seems bureaucratic and hierarchical.

The postmodern skepticism toward systematic ideologies and universal categories has led many to explore local knowledge and local communities, rejecting visions of globalization and the world metropolis. We have shifted attention from the whole to the partial, from the mass to the individual, from the unitary to the fragmentary, from the vertical to the horizontal (Marcus 2012).

The New Left of the 1960s and 1970s foreshadowed this tendency with its concern for democratic participation in civic life. The Port Huron Statement of SDS in 1962 criticized American individualism, militarism, the Cold War, segregation and discrimination, and poverty, and called for a participatory democracy (Hayden 2013; J. Miller 1987). SDS was inspired by the fieldwork of SNCC in the South, where SNCC field staff began by gaining the trust of the local black community leaders (Carson 1981; Dittmer 1995; Hogan 2007; Payne 1995). Seeing themselves at first as a "band of brothers" living out the "beloved community," SNCC became a staff-run organization with thoroughly participatory decision-making (Polletta 1994: 50–2).

SDS started the Economic Research and Action Project (ERAP) in 1964, hoping to use community organizing projects in up to a dozen Northern cities to start an interracial movement of the poor, with the slogan "Let the People Decide!" That populist slogan assumes that a democratic process will select those issue campaigns that will develop leaders and build a powerful people's organization. The issue campaigns would be means rather than ends in themselves. Ideology-based campaigns, on the other hand, start with a vision and analysis of issues that are ends in themselves. In Chicago, ERAP built an organization called JOIN (Jobs or Income Now), based on an SDS analysis. Where ERAP let local communities decide their own issues, they often identified practical neighborhood problems, like adequate garbage collection – which was dubbed GROIN by an ERAP critic with a sense of humor: "Garbage Removal or Income Now." The tensions between ideological and popular direction, and student staff influence vs. community member control, were never resolved (Breines 1989).

By and large, ERAP had little lasting success engaging the poor in their communities, and, with the exception of Chicago and Newark, most of the projects were abandoned within a year or two (Breines 1989: 123–49; Sale 1994: 95–150). And after becoming the largest national student organization since the 1930s, SDS self-destructed in 1969 as the escalating opposition to the Vietnam War drove factions further and further to the Leninist left. The practice of participatory democracy would remain to be developed by the women's liberation movement and the movements using nonviolent direct action.

Women's Liberation and Women-Centered Approaches

After women won the vote with passage of the Nineteenth Amendment in 1920, the feminist movement seemed to fade from public consciousness. The lone exception was Alice Paul's National Women's Party, which had run a campaign of nonviolent direct action and civil disobedience for the woman suffrage amendment (Walton 2010). For the next 50 years Paul waged a persistent campaign for an Equal Rights Amendment – a small, elite, sectarian group facing a much larger set of women in government and the labor movement who favored protective legislation for working women (Rupp and Taylor 1987). Although the women's movement appeared to be in the doldrums, there were gains made: the Children's Bureau and the Women's Bureau in the Department of Labor offered opportunities for women. During the New Deal, Eleanor Roosevelt supported an informal network of women in the federal government, and a strong women's division was established within the Democratic National Committee.

During the Second World War "Rosie the Riveter" modeled the patriotic woman working in the defense industries. But with the end of the war in 1945, women were expected to give their jobs to male veterans and return to being homemakers. Although many did devote themselves to raising the baby-boom generation, more women were moving into the workforce, and getting college degrees in such fields as education, nursing, and social work. In 1961 Women's Bureau director Esther Peterson talked President John F. Kennedy into setting up the President's Commission on the Status of Women, chaired by Eleanor Roosevelt. Its 1963

133

report made mild recommendations to improve the situation of women. State commissions on the status of women were established, and at a national conference of state commissions in 1965, Betty Friedan proposed setting up a National Organization for Women. This became the establishment women's movement, seeking not to eliminate hierarchy, but to advance up the ladder within it.

Around the same time, radical feminists, reacting to their experience of male chauvinism in the civil rights movement and the New Left, began to meet and talk in small groups (Evans 1979). From these "consciousness-raising groups" emerged the decentralized women's liberation movement, with the slogans "the personal is political" and "sisterhood is powerful." During the 1970s radical feminists formed numerous local women's organizations, including rape crisis centers, shelters from domestic violence, health clinics, music festivals, bookstores, and newspapers.

The initial small groups generally operated without designated leaders or other structures of organization. That worked well for purposes of free and open conversation, but became problematic when more complicated projects were undertaken. As radical feminist Jo Freeman pointed out in her famous article "The Tyranny of Structurelessness" (first published under the pen name "Joreen"), "there is no such thing as a structureless group." The idea of a leaderless and structureless group

> becomes a smoke screen for the strong or the lucky to establish unquestioned hegemony over others. . . . the idea of "structurelessness" does not prevent the formation of informal structures, only formal ones. . . . Thus structurelessness becomes a way of masking power. . . . As long as the structure of the group is informal, the rules of how decisions are made are known only to a few. . . . for everyone to have the opportunity to be involved in a given group and participate in its activities, the structure must be explicit, not implicit. (Freeman 1973: 286–7)

Similarly, accountability is possible only if specific responsibilities have been delegated to specific people, and everyone is aware of who is responsible for what. These are the very issues Kristina Smock identified in her discussion of the women-centered model of community organization (Smock 2004: 248–61).

Nonviolent Direct Action and the Anti-Nuclear Movement

An intensive, small group form of participatory democracy revived with the renewal of opposition to nuclear power and nuclear weapons, beginning with the Clamshell Alliance founded in New Hampshire in 1976 to oppose building a nuclear power plant at Seabrook. Nonviolent direct action was organized in affinity groups for maximum small group autonomy and tactical innovation in rapidly changing circumstances.

Barbara Epstein's account in *Political Protest and Cultural Revolution* (1991) traces a history that includes the Abalone Alliance of northern California, which opposed the Diablo Canyon nuclear power plant, and the Livermore Action Group, which protested nuclear weapons research at the University of California's Lawrence Livermore Laboratory. Out of the direct action affinity groups emerged a prefigurative, utopian approach to politics that drew on a tradition that Epstein has called "anarcha-feminism" (Epstein 1991: 168). Many groups put as much emphasis on forming community as they did on taking action to stop nuclear power and weapons. Despite her sympathy for the direct action movement, Epstein concluded that the absolute equality the movement often aspires to is unrealistic and unworkable:

> The question of hierarchy, and its relation to an egalitarian movement and society, is also considerably more complex than the direct action movement often takes it to be. . . . No large organization can function unless some people make sure that it does. Preferably these people should not be self-appointed but should be responsible to the rest of the organization. The failure to acknowledge leadership, or to train new leaders to replace those who need to reduce their involvement, has created problems for each of the large direct action organizations. (Epstein 1991: 271; see also Becker 1978)

Seattle, Anti-Globalization, and the Global Justice Movement

Opposition to expanding international trade agreements had been led by organizations from the AFL-CIO to Ralph Nader's Trade Watch. The World Trade Organization (WTO) meeting in Seattle in December 1999 became a major focus for international protest. A coalition of labor and environmentalists – the so-called "Teamsters and Turtles" – called for demonstrations. It marked an early stage in a "blue–green alliance": cooperation between groups like the AFL-CIO and the Sierra Club. Civil disobedience was planned by the Direct Action Network; nuclear protest veterans brought their affinity group structure to attempt to stop the WTO meeting. Seattle marked the emergence of the anarchist Black Bloc – some of whom were followers of the "anarcho-primitivism" of John Zerzan of Portland, Oregon. The police were unprepared for the militancy of the crowds and overreacted toward peaceful demonstrators, resulting in the "Battle of Seattle."

Demonstrators went on to Washington, DC, to protest a meeting of the World Bank and the International Monetary Fund (IMF) in April 2000, followed by protests at the Democratic National Convention in Los Angeles in July and the Republican National Convention in Philadelphia in August. International protests took place at the IMF meeting in Prague in September, at a European Union Summit in Nice in December, at the Summit of the Americas in Quebec City in April 2001, and at the European Economic Summit in Salzburg in July. Violence escalated when the Group of 8, the G-8 industrial nations, met in Genoa in July 2001 to discuss global poverty; a riot ensued in which one demonstrator was killed. Then, two months later in September, came the 9/11 attacks on the World Trade Center in New York and the Pentagon in Washington, DC, by al-Qaida. A new atmosphere impacting perceptions of violence and terrorism served to dampen enthusiasm for protest.

Meanwhile, to counter the label of "anti-globalization," which made the protesters seem only negative with no positive program, the first World Social Forum was held in Puerto Alegre, Brazil, in January 2001, with the slogan "Another World is Possible," as a counter-cultural version of the World Economic Forum, which has met annually in Davos, Switzerland, since 1971. Also becoming an annual event, the World Social Forum found its participants unable to generate a common program. The impossibility of agreeing on a political platform is evident from a look at the various elements regularly attending the World Social Forums: indigenous groups, militant localists, unreconstructed communist and Trotskyist factions, 57 varieties of anarchists, some democratic socialists. In our postmodern era of multiple identities, and a renewed identification with local traditions, the appeal of a unitary and universal internationalism that could form the basis of a common political program has gained little traction. Although rebranded as part of a global justice movement, the event has become more of a global counter-cultural jamboree.

To reduce the burden of people having to travel to the far corners of the earth to attend, activists were urged to develop Social Forum events in their home countries. US Social Forums were held in Atlanta in June 2007 and in Detroit in June 2010. ACORN founder Wade Rathke spent a day and a half at the Detroit Social Forum; some comments from his report:

> Many can hardly tolerate the seeming chaos of the Social Forum structure or its aimlessness. There is no agenda and purpose larger than the exercise itself. . . . The workshops are self-organized, so their variety can be endless and range in attendance from nobody to overflowing crowds. . . . Rooms and venues change suddenly and inexplicably. . . . One has to applaud the effort and look past the product, since there will not be one. . . . my simple point is not that a social forum will show the future of organizing, but that there will be something to learn. . . . (Rathke 2010: 50–1)

Rathke's observations suggest that global justice activists have a variety of prefigurative politics that fit well with (and helped shape) the Occupy movement as it emerged in 2011.

The Occupy Movement

On the evening of September 17, 2011, a mixed group of demonstrators threw down their sleeping bags in Zuccotti Park in Lower Manhattan and proclaimed they were representing the 99 percent against the 1 percent. The reference was to economist Joseph Stiglitz's article in the May issue of *Vanity Fair*, "Of the 1%, by the 1%, for the 1%." At first the occupiers of the park received little notice, but with the first newspaper stories sympathetic crowds began coming to join them. Sociologist Todd Gitlin noted the surprising degree of support received by the demonstrators:

> Unlike any other movement on the American left in at least three-quarters of a century, this movement began with a majority base of support. . . .What it stood for – economic justice and curbs on the wealthy – was popular. . . . They could see that the point of the movement was to resist the grotesque inequalities that have become normal in American life. (Gitlin 2012: 33)

The example of Occupy Wall Street (OWS), as the Zuccotti Park protest became known, spread swiftly to cities across the country, possibly as many as 500 cities and towns having some Occupy presence within the next month or two, most with an encampment on public property. The slogan "We are the 99 percent" resonated immediately with a large proportion of the population, most of whom had been impacted in some way by the financial crisis and recession which had begun in 2007. OWS quickly displaced the attention the right-populist Tea Party had been getting in the mainstream media since its debut appearance at the Congressional town hall meetings on the Obama health plan held in the summer of 2009.

Occupy introduced a number of ritual practices, which served to establish a subcultural identity for participants in the movement. Decisions would be made in a general assembly at which anyone could speak, as often and as long as they wished, or so it seemed. Participants in a discussion would silently "twinkle" fingers to indicate agreement or applause. A variety of hand signals symbolized blocking consensus, disagreement without blocking, getting off topic, and so on. The people's microphone, in which the speaker would pause every 20 words or so and the crowd would repeat what the speaker had said, was a novel innovation. Calls of "Mike check!" were repeated whether the edges of the crowd could hear or not.

Case Study: Occupy Santa Rosa

OWS issued a call for a national day of marches on Saturday, October 15, 2011. The proposal got lots of support from unions, environmentalists, and other activist groups – much of it spurned by OWS. An estimated 100 communities held marches or demonstrations that day. In Sonoma County, California, where the author lives, some 2,750 people (twice the number expected by the organizers) turned out for a lively rally and march, complete with a drumming circle and a brass marching band. The event was co-sponsored by Occupy Santa Rosa (OSR) and MoveOn's Sonoma County Council, despite warnings from OWS that MoveOn was trying to co-opt the Occupy movement (Gitlin 2012: 145–50). It was the sixth largest rally in the country that day, according to the *New York Times*, behind only New York, Los Angeles, San Francisco, Portland, and Seattle – and ahead of Chicago, Philadelphia, and Washington, DC.

The initial Santa Rosa Occupy group, consisting of five young people (four in their twenties), had met each other for the first time just 12 days before. Each was skilled in social media and had created his or her own Facebook or web page for a prospective Occupy Santa Rosa. I caught a note of their planning to work together, and I asked to join them at their first face-to-face meeting on behalf of the MoveOn Sonoma County Council, for which I was volunteering as council coordinator. Most of the group was new to local left politics, and had few connections to labor, peace, environmental, and social justice activists. I suggested we merge MoveOn's plans for a "Jobs Not Cuts!" rally on October 15 with the Occupy call. They would handle most of the publicity, and I would pull together local speakers for the rally, with their approval.

Planning meetings were held every couple of days, with the circle of local activists involved rapidly expanding. Our district Congresswoman, Lynne Woolsey, then co-chair of the Congressional Progressive Caucus, offered to make a speech, or send an aide with her message, but Occupy didn't want any elected officials speaking at the event. We ended up with six local speakers, well balanced (three men, three women; three Anglos, three Latinos; three young, three older) and representing labor and social justice organizations. A young woman from the initial OSR group of five served as MC for the rally. The unexpected success of the event left the OSR core group elated and optimistic, but – as the future would show – this turned out to have been the high point of OSR's public support.

The trajectory of OSR paralleled the experience of many local Occupy efforts around the country. An initial daily presence of Occupy tables and pickets on the sidewalks outside City Hall drew public sympathy as people stopped by with food and other supplies for the two dozen to 100 people maintaining the vigil. The City Council itself remained sympathetic until OSR decided to put up tents and maintain a 24-hour presence on the lawns in front of City Hall. Marches to protest banks' foreclosure policies were held on Saturdays, along with campaigns to "move your money" to local banks and credit unions. Working groups were formed for various causes, and one, termed "Legalize Sleep!" – to revoke a city ordinance prohibiting homeless people from sleeping in cars or in the parks – initially did not win support from a majority of the City Council. But two years later, when joined by more moderate advocates for the homeless, special parking areas were established for homeless people living out of their cars.

Occupy's refusal to engage with electoral politics did nothing to increase its credibility with the City Council. Nightly general assemblies went on for hours with little decided. OSR refused to set an end date to their tent city, and the scene was getting more problematic. Campers gradually separated into two factions: the political idealists on the west lawn, and the homeless and druggies on the east lawn, who began to call their camp "South Central" and the politicos' camp "West LA" – a sly reference to Los Angeles' inner city and the privileged west side. Public attitudes toward Occupy were influenced by the more disruptive demonstrations in San Francisco and Oakland, where a call for a November 5 general strike had managed to shut down the Port of Oakland for a day. Small groups of pro-testers had smashed windows and thrown rocks at police, and proponents of a "diversity of tactics" debated with adherents of strict nonviolence. The Santa Rosa City Council implemented a 15-day permit process that covered about half the 100 tents on site. Unpermitted tents were removed by police just before Thanksgiving. As conditions continued to deteriorate, the Council had the rest of the encampment removed before Christmas 2011.

Freed from the problems of the encampment, it appeared that OSR might be able to launch a number of promising campaigns in 2012. A Free School working group held regular educational programs on a variety of topics. In May, a national campaign, "The 99 Percent Spring," held a teach-in on nonviolent direct action. MoveOn was the lead sponsor locally; OSR did not endorse the training program, but several Occupy activists were among the 80 people attending the training. By the summer, however, all the original five initiators of OSR had dropped out. Many OSR participants grew increasingly frustrated with the general assembly meetings. A spokescouncil was set up to meet weekly, with a spokesperson from each of the working groups. A monthly general assembly meeting would be the ultimate decision-making body.

OSR had great expectations that a one-year anniversary march to be held in October 2012 would revitalize the Occupy movement. However, only 200 people turned out, less than 10 percent of the crowd a year before. The Occupy movement had failed to discover how to engage and organize that initial crowd that had mobilized at the start of the movement. We can only speculate about an explanation, but surely it was some combination of lack of clarity about objectives, confusion about tactics, absence of a credible long-range strategy, the cumbersome and interminable meetings, acrimonious disputes among the *de facto* leadership that had prompted many of the early leaders to quit the movement in disillusionment, and in general a process of decision-making that disadvantaged anyone not young and unemployed. As the second anniversary of Occupy approached, Nathan Schneider (2013) wrote in *The Nation* that "a sense of failure" pervaded the movement.

Occupy and American anarchism   Although much of OWS and many of its imitators across the United States had the appearance of being a novel and spontaneous happening, to a few veteran champions of direct democracy and direct action this was a clear program of principled anarchism. Anthropologist David Graeber is one of the foremost theorist-activists of Occupy. Anarchism, he wrote, is "a social movement with deep roots in American history, founded above all on an opposition to all structures of systematic coercion and a vision of a society based on principles of voluntary association, mutual aid and autonomous, self-governing communities" (Graeber 2000: 18). Elsewhere he expressed his reaction to the Occupy movement as follows: "For 'small-a' anarchists such as myself – that is, the sort willing to work in broad coalitions as long as they work on horizontal principles – this is what we'd always dreamed of" (Graeber 2013: 89).

Graeber sees Occupy as an example of prefigurative politics, "the idea that the organizational form that an activist group takes should embody the kind of society we wish to create" (Graeber 2013: 23). With prefigurative politics, "action itself becomes prophecy" (Graeber 2013: 233). Graeber's effort to use the Occupy model as the basis of a society-wide transformation, however, seems a reach too far: ". . . the Occupy movement is ultimately based on what in revolutionary theory is often called a dual power strategy: we are trying to create liberated territories outside of the existing political, legal, and economic order, on the principle that that order is irredeemably corrupt" (Graeber 2013: 259). To insist that the existing order is "irredeemably corrupt" makes it very difficult to find significant allies to work with. Occupy resisted listing its demands or stating exactly what it was for in specific terms, leaving sociologist Todd Gitlin to think "the movement could come to feel that its primary achievement was itself – a sort of collective narcissism" (Gitlin 2012: 94). Jonathan Matthew Smucker, a shrewd participant in and observer of the Occupy movement, noted the hazards of that stance:

> The big danger is that radical subcultures caught in this pattern of emphasizing how different they are may, over time, start to even prize their own marginalization. . . . If society is bad, then marginalization in society may be seen as good. We may tell each other stories of how we were ostracized in this or that group, how we're the outcast in our family, how we were the only revolutionary in a group of liberal reformists, etc. We may begin to swim in our own marginalization. This is the *story of the righteous few*. (Smucker 2012: 249, original italics)

Needless to say, a movement that claims to represent a solid majority of people does not want to be drawn into a narrative of the righteous few.

Richard Rothstein, in his essay "What is an Organizer?" written in 1974 for the Midwest Academy, makes a comment that can apply as readily 40 years later to Occupy:

> ... spontaneous militancy is rare in social life. When it happens, a spontaneous movement, a mass unplanned uprising, is very powerful. It is also very short-lived. . . . To build lasting political force on any issue requires not spontaneity but organization. It requires a slow process of leadership development. It requires the multiplication of leaders with a long term perspective, with the ability to plan strategy and the skill of marshaling forces at the right time in the right place. (Quoted in Schutz and Sandy 2011: 34)

Not every anarchist rejects organizing in this vein. A fascinating pamphlet by a Boston "anarcho-communist" identified only as "Dave," who became a community organizer to learn such skills as "building an organization, running campaigns, running meetings, doing turn-out and polarizing targets," argues that anarchists have a lot to learn from community organizing about engaging working-class people (Dave n.d.: 4).

In her conclusion to *Democracy in Action* (2004), Kristina Smock argues that her "women-centered model" (one version of horizontalism) can be effective in engaging the most disenfranchised. Its decision-making process is highly democratic and inclusive. The limits of the approach include its size and scale; it is best adapted to small groups and organizations. There is always a danger that process will be emphasized to the detriment of product.

For a useful guide to developing collaborative groups, see Starhawk's *The Empowerment Manual* (2011), which has guidelines for facilitating groups, leadership roles for leaderless groups, resolving conflict, and dealing with difficult people.

Asset-Based Community Development and Consensus Organizing

Between community organizing and community development are projects with some elements of both fields. In certain cases, the leading figures are people who began organizing within the Alinsky tradition, but moved to what they felt was a more effective and more comfortable formula for improving communities. Foremost among these intermediate positions are the "asset-based community development" (ABCD) of John McKnight and John Kretzmann, co-founders and co-directors of the Asset-Based Community Development Institute of the School of Education and Social Policy at Northwestern University, and the "consensus organizing" of Mike Eichler, a lecturer at San Diego State University's School of Social Work and founder and director of SDSU's Consensus Organizing Center.

Asset-Based Community Development

In his manifesto for ABCD, *The Careless Society: Community and Its Counterfeits* (1995), John McKnight has a chapter titled "Community Organizing in the Eighties: Toward a Post-Alinsky Agenda." McKnight grants that Alinsky was a giant in community organizing for his time, but times have changed. In Alinsky's day, McKnight asserts, poor and working-class neighborhoods contained vital organizations – "churches, ethnic groups, political organizations, and labor unions" (McKnight 1995: 154). Organizers could pull together leaders of these existing groups, identify local problems, and target the "enemy," who was outside the neighborhood but still available in the surrounding community. This formula worked for many years, and got results, but now the components of that strategy have deteriorated to the point that the approach no longer works, McKnight argues.

In addition, McKnight criticizes the professionalization of the human services and criminal justice systems for doing more harm than good for poor communities by labeling people by their deficiencies, problems, and pathologies. He denounces the therapeutic and the advocacy visions of society in favor of a community vision that builds on the strengths or "assets" of individuals within the community itself. John Kretzmann and McKnight have an excellent manual, *Building Communities from the Inside Out*

(1993), that provides a multitude of ideas about how to develop individual and institutional capacities of poor and working-class communities.

Mike Miller (2009b) criticizes McKnight's description of Alinsky's approach by pointing out that Alinsky clearly saw the need for a national network of people's organizations to take on those issues that can only be resolved at the national level. The local self-help projects Kretzmann and McKnight advocate are well and good in themselves, but depend on some level of outside funding. Their program has no clear plan for its own national network to protect such funding – leaving them at the mercy of a different layer of dependency of sources far from the local community. Without organizing for political power, the self-help approach is dependent on the goodwill of the defenders of the status quo, and is defenseless against shifts they may make to protect their interests.

In his recent book with Peter Block, *The Abundant Community* (2012), McKnight critiques the shift from citizen to consumer, and argues for rejecting consumer society in favor of a community of citizens. Our families, neighborhoods, and communities have the gifts, skills, and capacities to create abundance. The critical role is not the organizer or leader, but the "connector," who brings people together in new forms of association (McKnight and Block 2012: 115–48).

Consensus Organizing

Mike Eichler says he began as a community organizer in the Alinsky tradition because he was "predisposed . . . to distrust the rich and powerful" (Eichler 2007: 26). He changed his mind after some positive cooperative experiences, including a project in Pennsylvania's Monongahela Valley, in which all parties agreed on a goal and worked together to achieve it. Eichler's approach of finding mutual self-interest makes sense for someone working in the social service bureaucracy, whether public or private nonprofit, who is given an assignment that involves cooperation among a number of organizations of various types – in other words, for someone in the human services bureaucracy criticized by John McKnight. Although it borrows tools from the Alinsky tradition of community organizing – such as the one-on-one – consensus organizing has the feel of a Dale Carnegie approach ("how to win friends and influence people") to succeeding as a human services staffer. It has little or nothing to do with building a people's power organization. An Alinsky tradition organizer would argue that consensus is best reached not by flattery but through negotiation from a position of power.

From a long-range perspective, there can be complementarity between conflict-accepting community organizing and consensus-oriented community development. Randy Stoecker, professor of sociology and moderator of COMM-ORG, the online conference on community organizing and development, sees a "bad cop–good cop" relationship between the two approaches: "Community organizing fights to change power relationships while community development focuses on operationalizing the benefits that come from changed power relationships" (Stoecker 2010). Recognizing this potential mutuality might cut down on the sniping between advocates of these two distinct approaches.

8

What's Next?

Having surveyed the state of community organizing today, what can we say about its future – or possible futures? Let's begin by summing up the present situation. Several new directions are apparent, including electoral work integrated with community organizing, developing a vision of transformative change that brings us closer to that "world as it should be," and forming community–labor alliances that build upon labor's renewed interest in the power that can be gained from working in coalition with community groups.

The number of IBCOs is at an all-time high of around 200. These institutions engage the volunteer service of some 2,900 board members and 600 paid staff. This figure does not include another set of community organizations built around individual memberships. The IBCOs are composed of approximately 3,500 religious congregations and some 1,000 other groups, including labor unions, public schools, neighborhood associations, and other advocacy groups. The majority of IBCOs are part of federated networks, three of which – the IAF, PICO, and Gamaliel – function on a national level, and several additional networks work on a regional level – including DART in the Southeast and Ohio River Valley; the InterValley Project in New England; regional congregations and neighborhood organizations focused on urban and low-income African American communities; the Western Organization of Resource Councils in the Northern Great Plains; and the Alliance for a Just Society, primarily in the Northwest (Wood et al. 2013).

The IBCOs are doing well overall, crossing racial and religious boundaries, with 13 percent of member institutions predominantly Latino, 30 percent predominantly African American, and 10 percent predominantly mixed non-white. More than 50 percent of IBCO staff organizers and board members are non-white. In a historic shift, over half the organizer staff (55 percent) are now women. Organizers are also a younger group, with a majority in 2011 between the ages of 20 and 40, as compared to 1999, when the majority was between 30 and 50. The core religious groups in the IBCOs remain the Mainline Protestant, Catholic, and Black Protestant congregations, although Jewish and Unitarian Universalist congregations are more evident now than earlier. Islamic mosques are occasionally represented. Evangelical and Pentecostal congregations remain substantially under-represented (Wood et al. 2013).

From this base of IBCOs that have had considerable success bridging race, religion, gender, class, and geography has grown a strategic capacity with the potential to help create democratic change on the local, regional, state, and national levels. Ten years ago, only 20 percent of IBCOs attempted to influence policy on the state level, and virtually none worked on the national level. Presently 25 percent work on such national issues as immigration, health care, housing, minimum or living wages, and public transportation.

Robert Fisher and Sally Tamarkin (2009) have recently argued that four strategic trends with conservative implications are dominating community organizing in the United States. These trends are, first, "a turn to culture"; second, "romanticizing the local"; third, a "turn to community building"; and, fourth, "disconnecting community organizing from social movements." This may have been the case 10 years ago, but only the first of these appears to be borne out by the evidence presented in this book, and it's not clear that an exclusive focus on economic issues would be a good idea. IBCOs with national network affiliations are certainly dealing with issues of economic inequality. An emphasis on culture can lead to process overshadowing productive action, particularly with congregation-based organizing, but for the most part that has not been a debilitating problem. Contrary to "romanticizing the local," we have documented a strong trend to dealing with issues at the metropolitan, regional, state, and national levels. The "turn to community building," using "asset-based" and other such strategies, seems no stronger now than it has always been – a temptation for long-established organizations without fresh leadership to turn to community development approaches. And finally, on the separation from social movements, we see an increased outreach to partnerships with unions, environmentalists, immigration reformers, and other advocacy groups. The IAF may maintain its traditional put-downs of movement activism, but the trend to find new allies and explore new progressive alignments is stronger than ever.

Integrated Voter Engagement

The basic concept of voter engagement is that "voters need to be contacted and involved between elections and not just during elections" (Pastor et al. 2013: 1–2). The challenge is to ensure that electoral moments become part of building lasting movements. One way of viewing this activity is to see it as Marshall Ganz envisioned with his Camp Obama training organizers for the 2008 Presidential campaign: canvassers would develop a relationship with the people they met going door-to-door, and keep them in touch with a permanent independent organization, both before and after the election. (As we saw in the preceding chapter, OFA did not achieve real independence from the Democratic National Committee or the White House.) *Integrated* voter engagement (IVE) refers here to the development of a symbiotic connection between the deep relationships of community organizing activity and the scaled-up number of contacts made through electoral canvassing and other campaign activities. "Integration" of grassroots leadership development and winning elections requires a delicate balancing act between long-range organizing and the time-limited electoral campaign. After the campaign, the task continues of turning voter lists contacts to new leadership for the organization.

149

Manuel Pastor and colleagues point out the difference between transient "moments" and longer-range "movements":

> Moments – such as the election of our first Black president in 2008, the mass immigrant rights mobilizations in 2006, the emergence of the Occupy movement . . . can create openings for public dialogue, temporarily shift the debate, and even catalyze concrete change in the moment. However, they do not necessarily hold people to a strategy, course of action, belief system, or set of values – and gains that are achieved (solely) in the moment are easily eroded and rolled back if there is no organized power and commitment to sustain them. The hard work of organizing – building strong leadership and an informed base at the ground level – must happen between the big moments in order to weave together a sustained movement. (Pastor et al. 2013: 24)

Several state-based groups have incorporated IVE into their organizing work, including Florida New Majority, California Calls, the Ohio Organizing Collaborative, and Virginia New Majority. Results of their IVE work have included "increased voter registration and turnout, heightened awareness about election issues, and getting more 'unlikely voters' to the polls" (Pastor et al. 2013: 10). Much of the IVE work has involved alliances between community organizing groups and labor unions – the Service Employees International Union in particular. Tensions arise in such partnerships from the advantages unions often have in staffing and funding electoral campaigns, top-down leadership versus grassroots mobilization, and maintaining grassroots connections between electoral campaigns. Substantial energy needs to be devoted to building trust among coalition partners.

Bridging Power and Vision

One of the consequences of the pragmatic and non-ideological character of the Alinsky tradition has been a very limited vision of what the "world as it should be" might look like. Emphasizing constant action on issues, according to one group of critics, has the consequence "that the educational dimensions . . . that contribute to the long-term vision, can be lost. A balance between organizing, mobilizing, and education can lift the necessity of always looking for the next issue and help build critical analytical leadership" (DeFilippis et al. 2010: 180). One solution to this challenge is a partnership of IBCOs with popular educators.

Kristina Smock (2004), summarizing the distinctive contributions of the five models in her classification system, notes that the *power-based model* (the Alinsky tradition) builds strong organizations and impacts public policy-making. The trade-off is a decision-making process that is delegated and does not involve all members directly. Moreover, local organizations must have links to other groups on a national scale if they are to make structural changes in our economy or society. In contrast, her *transformative model* challenges dominant ideological frameworks, and builds the foundation for deep change, but seldom has the clout to make change and achieve concrete results. Together, people-power organizations and popular education groups can provide the instruments for structural reform or transformative change.

Smock writes that power-based organizations bring to movement alliances "large grassroots memberships, strong cores of skilled and experienced public leaders, and reliable sources of both internal and external funding" (Smock 2004: 238–9). In order to catalyze the social movement-generating potential of this IBCO infrastructure, "the funding structure for community organizing must adjust to reflect the importance of the informal cultural laboratories that provide the ideological foundation for movement building." Most importantly, Smock argues:

> Adherents of both the power-based and transformative models must set aside their turf wars and philosophical disagreements long enough to begin a dialogue about the potential for creating a complementary, synergistic relationship. . . . Power-based and transformative organizations should continue to operate independently from one another, but they should find ways to coordinate their efforts, working . . . toward the formation of a broad, unified social justice movement. (Smock 2004: 240)

IBCOs can develop a sense of their place in the history of social movements as well as formulate their long-term strategy and vision in association not only with well-established institutions of popular education like the Highlander Center, but also such smaller think-tanks and consultants as the Grassroots Policy Project which assist movement groups to develop power analysis, a progressive worldview, issue framing, electoral engagement, and strategy development (Healey and Hinson 2005).

Working Together

San Francisco organizer Mike Miller has been arguing for over 20 years that to achieve fundamental change in the United States, it will be necessary to "build autonomous, deeply rooted, broadly based, multi-issue, people-power organizations that can act locally and work together in larger political and economic arenas" (Miller 1993: 54). Recently he has suggested possible models for such cooperation:

> We can imagine a national federation of community organizations –
> analogous to the AFL-CIO, but with deeper levels of member
> participation – adopting a multi-issue economic and social justice
> agenda. ... Who will push community organizing in this direction?
> I don't think it will be the old generation of professional organizers.
> Rather it will be younger organizers, religious leaders of the major
> faiths that fund and legitimize organizing, local leaders seeking more
> cooperation among the networks right now, and sympathetic public
> intellectuals who recognize the contribution that community organ-
> izing has to make. (Miller 2010: 48)

In September 2013 AFL-CIO president Richard Trumka proposed that the labor federation admit groups other than unions as members or affiliates, mentioning specifically the Sierra Club, the NAACP, and the National Council of La Raza. The alliance would bring more clout to efforts to increase the minimum wage, improve workplace safety, and increase taxes on the wealthy. It would also serve as a political counterweight to corporate America and conservative billionaires (Greenhouse 2013b). Trumka's proposal is another step in moving forward a strategy of broad progressive coalition development by the labor movement to develop and extend a model of regional power building. Examples include such California groups as Working Partnerships USA, the Los Angeles Alliance for a New Economy (LAANE), and Strategic Concepts in Organizing and Policy Education (SCOPE), as Amy Dean and David Reynolds have described (Dean and Reynolds 2009: 39–83). Although unions were part of Alinsky's early people's organizations, the emphasis for many years on congregation-based community organizing has given unions only a minor role and presence at best. Today, as membership is declining in just those denominations that have been the mainstays of IBCOs, the need to broaden the base of community organizations is matched by the willingness of certain unions at least to join such ecumenical efforts.

With the decline of union membership, labor has been experimenting with new forms of organizing the working poor, many of which can be natural partners or members of IBCOs. Workers' centers are one such form, often comprised of undocumented immigrants and other low-wage workers. They generally combine the functions of service delivery, advocacy, English language instruction, leadership development, and other activities once provided by settlement houses. Another form would be day labor centers, which help maintain uniform higher wage levels in the informal sector, and protect undocumented workers from wage theft by unscrupulous employers (Greenhouse 2013a; Milkman 2012). The National Day Labor Organizing Network was founded in 2001 to support local groups and impact federal and state policy.

Community–labor coalitions are another hybrid form that brings together labor and community groups in a spirit reminiscent of the CIO organizing drives of the 1930s, like the Back of the Yards campaign to organize the packinghouse workers that inspired Alinsky's first community organizing effort. Such coalitions also draw on the work done in California's San Joaquin

Valley by Cesar Chavez and Fred Ross, Sr. building the UFW with various kinds of community backing, ranging from boycotts and strike support to demonstrations and fundraising. Recent community–labor coalitions have included assistance to Justice for Janitors campaigns, living wage and minimum wage movements, and community benefit agreements (CBAs). The Staples Center CBA in Los Angeles is an excellent example of providing training and local hires for construction jobs. Amy Dean and Wade Rathke (2008) argue that such coalitions need to move from ad hoc arrangements through mutual support coalitions to deep coalitions that can build political power.

One effort to standardize a structure for community–labor coalitions is Jobs with Justice (JwJ), a national network of local coalitions whose members are labor unions, religious congregations, community organizations, and student groups. JwJ was founded in 1987 to support working people by building long-term coalitions with the power to win reforms in such areas as labor law, health care, union organizing, and immigrant rights. Local chapters of JwJ have a minimum of five unions and five community groups as members. Individual members of local JwJ coalition partners are asked to pledge to turn out at least five times a year in support of actions in solidarity with working people's struggles. To encourage a stronger common organizing culture, JwJ recently initiated a training program for its local coalitions that draws on the Alinsky tradition trainings. JwJ merged with American Rights at Work in 2012. There are JwJ coalitions in 46 cities in 28 states (Larson 2013).

The response of the major national CBCO networks to the potential of broadening their base beyond congregation members has varied. The IAF has generally stood aloof from more than a token representation of unions, although it has school members where it has major programs of educational reform. The IAF has worked on state-level policy, but in general has left federal policy lobbying to its affiliates in the mid-Atlantic and Northeastern states, now under the umbrella of Metro IAF. PICO National Network is almost exclusively congregation-based, but it is very willing to work in coalition with other groups on state and national issues. The Gamaliel Foundation has been perhaps most willing to encourage incorporating secular groups in its affiliates, and to work in coalition with a variety of unions and other advocacy groups. Among the regional networks, most are either congregation-based like DART, or largely secular.

Although they have been notoriously competitive, it is high time the IBCO networks began to collaborate with each other on regional, state, and national policy objectives.

Over the Long-Range: Toward a Progressive Strategic Alignment

In a general sense, strategy is planning and directing a program of action to reach the most advantageous position prior to engaging an opponent. To assemble a majoritarian coalition would require a broad range of IBCOs, unions, and advocacy groups, and other SMOs. It wouldn't be easy: choosing power over protest would be a shift for SMOs long unconcerned with actually winning – where mobilizing protest is easier than organizing for long-haul policy victories, and self-expression is preferred to compromise. Groups with a strong ideological commitment may have difficulty with a focus on interests, values, and the pursuit of winnable objectives – reflecting the old debate about reform (and co-optation) vs. revolutionary purity (and sectarianism). There is, however, a growing appetite for such a combined movement. Fifteen years ago a "listening project" among organizers and activists undertaken by the Peace Development Fund (1999) found most seeking a common strategic vision that could overcome fragmentation of the progressive movement. More recently a survey of community organizers on the left showed that a vast majority of veteran organizers are eager to develop a new common vision, end self-marginalization, and help form a "movement of movements" (Lee and Williams 2013).

Such a strategy means getting beyond the "headquarters-based coalition," in which the Washington office directors get together, draw up a list of points of agreement, shake hands, and declare a new alliance. A recent example is the full page of organizational logos attached to the call for training in nonviolent direct action for the "99 Percent Spring" in 2012. For the few groups that had a grassroots base, the word had not reached the local level by the time of the training. Many local trainers were frustrated that it was news to numerous union locals and environmental groups that they were collaborating in this effort. Making an alliance a real joint project on the local level is a difficult matter, requiring much greater commitment of resources to communicating with, training, and mentoring local organizers and leaders so the message reaches the grassroots base.

Many aspects of contemporary community organizing remain to be documented and analyzed. Community organizing has been an overwhelmingly urban phenomenon, and we have only a few studies of the challenges facing organizers in rural areas (Fisher 1993; Fisher and Smith 2012; Szakos and Szakos 2008; Wellstone 1978). The Alinsky tradition has taken root internationally, with the three national networks – the IAF, PICO, and Gamaliel – providing various degrees of support to community organizations in Canada, the United Kingdom, Australia, South Africa, Rwanda, Central America, and Germany (Baumann 2011; Rathke 2011a). ACORN International, meanwhile, has 11 affiliates in countries outside the United States. However, we are lacking comparative studies of how well approaches developed in the United States work in other countries.

The world of community organizing faces several great challenges. Organizers and leaders need to learn the history of movements for a more democratic and just social, economic, and political world, and situate community organizing within them. We need to build alliances – or at least "alignments" – with those groups that share many of our interests and values, including labor, environmentalists, and advocates for people of color, women, people with disabilities, and others. Organizers, leaders, and members need to give greater substance to a vision of "the world as it should be." Finally, we need to develop a strategy for moving closer to that world. This will be a lengthy process indeed. But the demographic tides are running in favor of a progressive alignment in the United States (Judis and Teixeira 2004). By itself, demography is not destiny. It will take human agency passionately committed to a democratic and just outcome. As for me, in the interim I join organizer Mary Gonzales in choosing a society of "shared abundance, not scarcity; community, not isolation; and hope, not despair."

Acknowledgements

Writing this book brings my work with community organizing full circle, bridged in mid-career by academic studies of social movements. Individuals named in the following narrative include mentors, supervisors, colleagues, and friends to whom I owe many debts of gratitude. There are many others of course, but I've focused on those with the most direct connection to the subject of this book.

San Francisco organizer Mike Miller appears both at the beginning and at the end of my chronology of indebtedness (see Miller 2009a). During my sophomore year at the University of California, Berkeley (1960–1), Mike organized me into my first venture in political action – accompanying and driving fellow members of our campus political party, SLATE (see Miller 2000), to campaign at residence halls, co-ops, fraternities, and sororities for election to the board of the Associated Students. By the next year I was campaigning as a candidate myself. SLATE was known for great parties (the other kind), often hosted by the expatriate Yugoslav radical Bogdan Denitch. At one of these I met Michael Harrington, the democratic socialist whose book *The Other America* (1962) moved me to get involved in the War on Poverty.

Heading to Washington, DC, after graduation at the end of spring 1964, I was rescued from an internship deep in an obscure unit of the Department of Health, Education, and Welfare by the memorable Vocational Rehabilitation director Mary Switzer, the *grande dame* of the federal bureaucracy, who stationed me in her outer office. From there I was recruited by Jule Sugarman in the spring of 1965 and put to work on the launch of Project Head Start at the Office of Economic Opportunity (OEO). Given the shortage of staff for the new agency, I spent a brief few weeks just before the summer programs began as the acting director of training for Head Start. This led me to the extraordinary experience of visiting the Child Development Group of Mississippi (CDGM) in the summer of 1965 for its training program and the first week of poor black Mississippians running their own preschool program (see Dittmer 1995: 363–88; Greenberg 1990). In the fall Richard Boone (author of the mandate for "maximum feasible participation" of the poor in Community Action Programs) in CAP's research and demonstration office assigned me to work with college student volunteer programs, including TICEP at Tuskegee Institute in Alabama, health science students in California's Central Valley and inner-city ghettoes, and the Appalachian Volunteers (AVs) in the coalfields of eastern Kentucky and southern West Virginia.

After taking off six months for travel in 1966, I was debating rejoining the bureaucracy in Washington when an invitation came from AVs director Milton Ogle to join their community organizing staff in eastern Kentucky. I took the leap, and found myself celebrating my 25th birthday in an abandoned, dilapidated coal camp commissary in Harlan County, Kentucky. I began with the thought I might give it a year, but stayed with the AVs from the fall of 1966 until the organization's demise in the spring of 1970, serving as the executive director during the AVs' final year (see Walls 2009–10). During that time I became acquainted with Myles Horton at the Highlander Center, which had relocated to Knoxville, and later New Market, Tennessee, as we brought Appalachian grassroots leaders to workshops at Highlander.

I began graduate studies in sociology at the University of Kentucky (UK) in the fall of 1969, and moved to Lexington in 1970. I was hoping to find the time and the intellectual tools to digest and understand my experiences with the AVs. Once we started helping small farmers and landowners to oppose stripmining, the AVs had been hit by a political hailstorm, which included one member of our staff being charged with sedition, followed by an investigation by the Kentucky UnAmerican Activities Committee (KUAC – an unfortunate acronym that we pronounced as "quack"). Despite many shortcomings, measured against today's standards for organizing, the AVs managed to have some long-range impacts on the coalfield region, a balance I attempted to strike in a keynote at the 2011 conference of the Appalachian Studies Association, which hosted an AV reunion (Walls 2011).

I owe much to several inspiring and supportive professors at UK as well as my fellow graduate student colleagues who formed Collective One. The women in our collective were among the initiators (they wouldn't have liked the term "leaders") of the women's liberation movement at UK. I appreciate their patience in raising my consciousness, and for introducing me to Eleanor Flexner's classic *Century of Struggle* (1959), which greatly extended my understanding of the time horizon for social change.

One evening, probably in the spring of 1971, I drove to the University of Louisville to hear Saul Alinsky speak about the difficulties and the promise that the middle class presented for the coalition he was working to assemble. I was amused by his raucous stories, and agreed with his strategy of alliance between middle and working classes, but was not particularly excited by his organizing tactics, what little I understood of what little he explained of them.

At UK John B. Stephenson, later president of Berea College, chaired my dissertation committee, co-edited *Appalachia in the Sixties* (Walls and Stephenson 1972) with me, and was a co-founder of the Appalachian Center at UK with me and others, including my friend and frequent collaborator sociologist Dwight Billings. Before I completed my dissertation, I received an unexpected invitation to join the faculty of the School of Social Work at UK. And thanks to the encouragement of a new dean, Ronda Connaway, I was able to add to my supervision of field placements in Appalachian Kentucky the teaching of such classes as social policy and community organization and planning.

In 1982, with wife and child, I accepted an offer to move back to northern California and work at Sonoma State University (SSU), where I was hired to direct the grants office and manage the Academic Foundation. Two years later I was appointed dean of the School of Extended Education. I shifted my academic focus from Appalachian studies to the study of social movements. After interviewing over a hundred leaders of national advocacy organizations, I wrote *The Activist's Almanac* (Walls 1993). My teaching emphasized multidisciplinary approaches in courses on the civil rights movement, the women's movement, and the environmental movement. After retiring from SSU in 2005, I worked for the Osher Lifelong Learning Institutes and taught a course at several universities in the Bay Area on what accounts for successful social movements.

At the invitation of editor Kathy Cone I had written several articles for *The Workbook*, the late lamented quarterly published in Albuquerque aimed at activists in the Southwest and Rocky Mountain states. One of these articles was a survey of community organizing activity for the magazine's twentieth anniversary in 1994. Following up on that article with plans to update it for my website, I interviewed John Baumann of PICO in Oakland in October 1996. Later that month during a trip to Chicago, I interviewed Ed Chambers at the Industrial Areas Foundation (IAF), Gale Cincotta and Shel Trapp at National People's Action, and Greg Galluzzo at the Gamaliel Foundation. I feel fortunate to have met these pioneers in the field of community organizing, and I appreciate their generosity with their scarce time. In July 2001 the National Organizers Alliance held its Gathering at SSU, giving me the opportunity to meet many organizers not employed in the major networks and hear Tim Sampson and Anne Braden on a panel of "firestarters."

Meanwhile, after moving back to Sonoma County in 1982, one of my first friends in the community beyond the university was Larry Ferlazzo, then the young operator of the Catholic Worker Kitchen in Santa Rosa. Wanting to find a means of empowering the poor, he left the county for a three-year apprenticeship with the Alinsky-tradition IAF, to return as the initial organizer for the Sonoma County Faith-Based Organizing Project in 1988. The

project included 25 churches by 1991, and was building a powerful reputation. I watched the project with great interest, but was
too busy with my university job to be closely involved.

Ferlazzo moved on in 1993 to work with an IAF project in the
Sacramento Valley (he is now a master teacher in Sacramento),
and the project in Sonoma County began to founder, running
through two organizers. In 1997 it merged with an IAF effort in
Napa County to form the Sonoma–Napa Action Project (SNAP).
But SNAP fared no better, and soon disappeared from public view.
In late 2004 a North Bay Sponsoring Committee (NBSC) affiliated
with the IAF surfaced with an issues conference in Sonoma County
featuring an address by Ernesto Cortes, Jr. I attended as a member
of the Living Wage Coalition. Approaching retirement, I was
eager to see whether the vital organizing of a decade earlier could
be revived, and my friends and I could participate as members
of labor organizations. Apparently, however, the Sponsoring
Committee only wanted religious congregations as members, and
by the summer of 2005 it seemed to be making little progress.

Periodically over the next couple of years I'd have conversations
with Martin Bennett, a professor of American History at Santa
Rosa Junior College, about how much we in Sonoma County
needed an effective community organization in the Alinsky tradition. Then in February 2008 I got a telephone call from Michael
Jacoby Brown, an organizer and writer from the Boston area.
A wedding in his family was bringing him to Sonoma County.
He had read some of the social movement essays on my website
and wondered whether I'd be interested in calling a few people
together and he would talk about his recent book, *Building
Powerful Community Organizations* (2006).

I got a dozen people in my living room on a Sunday afternoon
for a house meeting with Brown, and we ended up talking about
how we should start building that new community organization.
As it turned out, half of the people attending Brown's talk became
part of the core group that launched the North Bay Organizing
Project (NBOP) planning process. So, thanks to Brown for cata-
lyzing our meeting, the tireless Marty Bennett for his persistence,
our talented and dedicated home-grown staff organizers Susan

Acknowledgements

Shaw and Davin Cardenas, and Una Glass and Bill Kortum, who brought in the environmental community.

By the summer of 2008 we were meeting regularly with the inspiring organizer and trainer Mary Gonzales and her husband Greg Galluzzo of the Gamaliel Foundation. I attended a six-day Gamaliel national leadership training at that time, and had the opportunity to be part of every step of building a broad-based community organization from the ground up. Since then I have attended and assisted in several half-day trainings led by Mary, and had innumerable hours of conversation with her and Greg about community organizing. And I have gotten to know Ana Garcia-Ashley, who became executive director of Gamaliel when Greg retired. Following the election of Barack Obama in the Presidential race of 2008, I became the volunteer council organizer for MoveOn.org in Sonoma County. I continued to volunteer with MoveOn until 2013, when it stopped supporting its face-to-face councils and turned to an online petition-promoting strategy. Our Sonoma County Council was one of the founding groups that formally established NBOP in 2010.

The idea for this book emerged after I was contacted by Polity for some comments on a series they were planning on social movements. I thought a book on community organizing would be a good addition to their series, and I suggested several possible authors. In the end, the editors asked me to submit a proposal. My thanks for the support from senior acquisitions editor Emma Longstaff, sociology editor Jonathan Skerrett, editorial assistant Elen Griffiths, copy-editor Justin Dyer, and production assistant India Darsley.

Despite my affiliations with Gamaliel, I have attempted to see it and other projects and networks clearly. Mike Miller, of the San Francisco-based Organize Training Center, remains a friend and mentor, and his comments have often compelled me to reconsider my thinking. Marty Bennett offered valuable suggestions, as did Aaron Schutz, Richard Massell, and two anonymous readers. I've looked at community organizing from inside as a volunteer and from outside as an academic researcher, and tried to be as objective as possible, given my own interests, values, and vision of

Acknowledgements

the better world I seek. If I have lapsed into bias or error, it's no one's responsibility but my own.

This book is dedicated to my wife and life partner Lucia, and to our grandchildren, in hope they will inherit a world closer to what it should be.

David Walls
Sebastopol, CA
March 2014

References

Adams, Frank (with Horton, Myles) (1975) *Unearthing Seeds of Fire: The Idea of Highlander*. Winston-Salem, NC: John F. Blair, Publisher.

Algren, Nelson (1951) *Chicago: City on the Make*. Garden City, NY: Doubleday.

Alinsky, Saul D. (1970) *John L. Lewis: An Unauthorized Biography*. New York: Vintage Books.

Alinsky, Saul D. (1972) *Rules for Radicals: A Pragmatic Primer for Realistic Radicals*. New York: Vintage Books.

Alinsky, Saul D. (1989) *Reveille for Radicals*. New York: Vintage Books.

Allsup, Carl (1982) *The American GI Forum: Origins and Evolution*. Austin: University of Texas Press.

Anderson, Jervis (1972) *A. Philip Randolph: A Biographical Portrait*. New York: Harcourt Brace Jovanovich.

Atlas, John (2010) *Seeds of Change: The Story of ACORN*. Nashville: Vanderbilt University Press.

Bailey, Jeff (1985) "Unlikely activist gets Chicago banks to give loans in poor sections." *Wall Street Journal*, August 21, pp. 1, 16.

Barber, Lucy G. (2002) *Marching on Washington: The Forging of an American Political Tradition*. Berkeley: University of California Press.

Bardacke, Frank (2011) *Trampling Out the Vintage: Cesar Chavez and the Two Souls of the United Farm Workers*. London and New York: Verso.

Baumann, John, S.J. (2011) "PICO: international organizing in Central America and Rwanda, Africa." *Social Policy*, Fall, pp. 33–5.

Becker, Norma (1978) "Beyond the abdication of power." *Win*, December 7, pp. 4–9.

Berger, Peter L. and Neuhaus, Richard John (1996) *To Empower People: From State to Civil Society*. Michael Novak, ed. Washington, DC: The AEI Press.

Betten, Neil and Austin, Michael J. (1990) *The Roots of Community Organizing, 1917–1939*. Philadelphia: Temple University Press.

References

Block, Stephanie (2012a) *Change Agents: Alinskyian Organizing among Religious Bodies, Vol. 1: A Brief History*. Madison: Spero Publishing.

Block, Stephanie (2012b) *Change Agents: Alinskyian Organizing among Religious Bodies, Vol. 2: Systemic Reform*. Madison: Spero Publishing.

Block, Stephanie (2012c) *Change Agents: Alinskyian Organizing among Religious Bodies, Vol. 3: Ideology*. Madison: Spero Publishing.

Block, Stephanie (2012d) *Change Agents: Alinskyian Organizing among Religious Bodies, Vol. 4: Organizers*. Madison: Spero Publishing.

Bobo, Kim, Kendall, Jackie, and Max, Steve (2010) *Organizing for Social Change: Midwest Academy Manual for Activists*, 4th edn. Santa Ana, CA: The Forum Press.

Boyte, Harry C. (1980) *The Backyard Revolution: Understanding the New Citizen Movement*. Philadelphia: Temple University Press.

Boyte, Harry C. (1984) *Community Is Possible: Repairing America's Roots*. New York: Harper & Row.

Boyte, Harry C. (1989) *CommonWealth: A Return to Citizen Politics*. New York: The Free Press.

Boyte, Harry C. and Riessman, Frank, eds. (1986) *The New Populism: The Politics of Empowerment*. Philadelphia: Temple University Press.

Boyte, Harry, Booth, Heather, and Max, Steve (1986) *Citizen Action and the New Populism*. Philadelphia: Temple University Press.

Breines, Wini (1989) *Community and Organization in the New Left, 1962–1968: The Great Refusal*. 2nd edn. New Brunswick, NJ: Rutgers University Press.

Brinkley, Douglas (2000) *Rosa Parks*. New York: Viking Penguin.

Brown, Michael Jacoby (2006) *Building Powerful Community Organizations: A Personal Guide to Creating Groups That Can Solve Problems and Change the World*. Arlington, MA: Long Haul Press.

Buechler, Steven M. (1995) "New social movement theories." *The Sociological Quarterly*, Vol. 36, No. 5, pp. 441–64.

Buechler, Steven M. (2004) "The strange career of strain and breakdown theories of collective action." In David A. Snow, Sarah A. Souke, and Hanspeter Kriesi, eds., *The Blackwell Companion to Social Movements*. Oxford: Blackwell Publishing.

Bulmer, Martin (1984) *The Chicago School of Sociology: Institutionalization, Diversity, and the Rise of Sociological Research*. Chicago: University of Chicago Press.

Burt, Kenneth C. (2007) *The Search for a Civic Voice: California Latino Politics*. Claremont, CA: Regina Books.

Campaign for Human Development (1995) "1994–95 Annual Report." Washington, DC: Campaign for Human Development.

Carawan, Guy and Carawan, Candie (1993) "Sowing on the mountain: nurturing cultural roots and creativity for community change." In Stephen L. Fisher, ed., *Fighting Back in Appalachia: Traditions of Resistance and Change*. Philadelphia: Temple University Press.

References

Carson, Clayborne (1981) *In Struggle: SNCC and the Black Awakening of the 1960s.* Cambridge, MA: Harvard University Press.

Chambers, Edward T. (1978) "Organizing for family and congregation." Franklin Square, NY: Industrial Areas Foundation.

Chambers, Edward T. (2004) *Roots for Radicals: Organizing for Power, Action, and Justice.* New York: Continuum.

Collins, Gail (2012) *As Texas Goes . . .: How the Lone Star State Hijacked the American Agenda.* New York: Liveright Publishing.

Coursey, Chris (2011) "Feeling the connection." *The Press Democrat,* October 26. *http://www.pressdemocrat.com/article/20111026/news/111029638.* Last accessed May 2, 2014.

Cruz, Wilfredo (1990) "UNO: organizing at the grassroots." In Peg Knoepfle, ed., *After Alinsky: Community Organizing in Illinois.* Springfield, IL: Sangamon State University Press.

Cryan, Phillip (n.d. [ca. 2012]) Strategic Practice for Social Transformation. Boston: Grassroots Policy Project.

Dahl, Robert (2005) *Who Governs? Democracy and Power in an American City.* 2nd edn. New Haven: Yale University Press.

Dave (n.d.) *The Intersections of Anarchism and Community Organising.* Fordsburg, South Africa: Zambalaza Books.

Dean, Amy and Rathke, Wade (2008) "Beyond the mutual backscratch: a new model for labor–community coalitions." *New Labor Review,* Fall, pp. 47–56.

Dean, Amy and Reynolds, David B. (2009) *A New New Deal: How Regional Activism Will Reshape the American Labor Movement.* Ithaca, NY: Cornell University Press.

DeFilippis, James, Fisher, Robert, and Shragge, Eric (2010) *Contesting Community: The Limits and Potential of Local Organizing.* New Brunswick, NJ: Rutgers University Press.

Delgado, Gary (1986) *Organizing the Movement: The Roots and Growth of ACORN.* Philadelphia: Temple University Press.

Delgado, Gary (1994) *Beyond the Politics of Place: New Directions in Community Organizing in the 1990s.* Oakland, CA: Applied Research Center.

Dittmer, John (1995) *Local People: The Civil Rights Struggle in Mississippi.* Urbana: University of Illinois Press.

Domhoff, G. William (2005) "Power at the local level: growth coalition theory." "Who Rules America?" website, April. *http://www2.ucsc.edu/whorules america/local/growth_coalition_theory.html.* Last accessed April 22, 2014.

Dreier, Peter (1975) "Power structures and power struggles." *The Insurgent Sociologist,* Vol. V, No. 3, Spring, pp. 233–44.

Dreier, Peter (2006) "Rosa Parks: angry, not tired." *Dissent,* Winter, pp. 88–92.

Dreier, Peter (2007) "Community organizing for what? Progressive politics and community building in America." In Marion Orr, ed., *Transforming the City:*

References

Community Organizing and the Challenge of Political Change. Lawrence: University Press of Kansas.

Dreier, Peter and Moberg, David (2008–9) "Community organizers: thank you, Sarah Palin." *Social Policy*, Fall, pp. 17–21.

Durr, Virginia (1985) *Outside the Magic Circle: The Autobiography of Virginia Foster Durr.* Hollinger F. Barnard, ed. Tuscaloosa: University of Alabama Press.

Easton, David (1968) *The Political System: An Inquiry into the State of Political Science.* New York: Knopf.

Eichler, Mike (2007) *Consensus Organizing: Building Communities of Mutual Self-Interest.* Thousand Oaks, CA: Sage Publications.

Elbaum, Max (2002) *Revolution in the Air: Sixties Radicals Turn to Lenin, Mao and Che.* London and New York: Verso.

Elshtain, Jean Bethke (2002) *Jane Addams and the Dream of American Democracy.* New York: Basic Books.

Epstein, Barbara (1991) *Political Protest and Cultural Revolution: Nonviolent Direct Action in the 1970s and 1980s.* Berkeley: University of California Press.

Evans, Sara (1979) *Personal Politics: The Roots of Women's Liberation in the Civil Rights Movement and the New Left.* New York: Random House.

Finks, P. David (1984) *The Radical Vision of Saul Alinsky.* Ramsay, NJ: Paulist Press.

Fisher, Robert (1994) *Let the People Decide: Neighborhood Organizing in America.* Updated edn. Boston: Twayne Publishers.

Fisher, Robert, ed. (2009) *The People Shall Rule: ACORN, Community Organizing, and the Struggle for Economic Justice.* Nashville: Vanderbilt University Press.

Fisher, Robert and Kling, Joseph M. (1987) "Leading the people: two approaches to the role of ideology in community organizing." *Radical America*, Vol. 21, No. 1, January–February, pp. 31–45.

Fisher, Robert and Tamarkin, Sally (2009) "Current trends in community organizing." *Social Policy*, Spring, pp. 48–50.

Fisher, Stephen L., ed. (1993) *Fighting Back in Appalachia: Traditions of Resistance and Change.* Philadelphia: Temple University Press.

Fisher, Stephen L. and Smith, Barbara Ellen, eds. (2012) *Transforming Places: Lessons from Appalachia.* Urbana: University of Illinois Press.

Flacks, Richard (2005) "The question of relevance in social movement studies." In David Croteau, William Hoynes, and Charlotte Ryan, eds., *Rhyming Hope and History.* Minneapolis: University of Minnesota Press.

Flanagan, Joan (1982) *The Grass Roots Fundraising Book.* Chicago: Contemporary Books.

Flanagan, Joan (2002) *Successful Fundraising: A Complete Handbook for Volunteers and Professionals.* New York: McGraw-Hill.

References

Flexner, Eleanor (1996) *Century of Struggle: The Woman's Rights Movement in the United States.* Enlarged edn. Cambridge, MA: Harvard University Press.

Freeman, Jo (1973) "The tyranny of structurelessness." In Anne Koedt, Ellen Levine, and Anita Rapone, eds., *Radical Feminism.* New York: Quadrangle Books.

Freire, Paulo (1968) *Pedagogy of the Oppressed.* Trans. Myra Bergman Ramos. New York: Herder and Herder.

Galluzzo, Greg (2009) "Community organizing through faith-based networks." In M. Paloma Pavel, ed., *Breakthrough Communities: Sustainability and Justice in the Next American Metropolis.* Cambridge, MA: MIT Press.

Gamaliel Foundation (2008) "Faith & Democracy: Executive Summary." Chicago: Gamaliel Foundation, Inclusion and Racial Equity Task Force, June 26.

Ganz, Marshall (2001) "The power of story in social movements." Kennedy School of Government, Harvard University, August. *http://citeseerx.ist.psu.edu/viewdoc/download?doi=10.1.1.94.1488&rep=rep1&type=pdf.* Last accessed May 2, 2014.

Ganz, Marshall (2009) *Why David Sometimes Wins: Leadership, Organization, and Strategy in the California Farm Worker Movement.* New York: Oxford University Press.

Ganz, Marshall (2010) "Leading change: leadership, organization and social movements." In Nitin Nohria and Rakesh Khurane, eds., *Handbook of Leadership Theory and Practice.* Cambridge, MA: Harvard Business School Press.

Ganz, Marshall and Wageman, Ruth (2008) "Sierra Club Leadership Development Project Report." May 8. Harvard University, Cambridge, MA. *http://leadingchangenetwork.com/files/2012/08/LDP-Final-Report.pdf.* Last accessed April 22, 2014.

Gecan, Michael (2002) *Going Public: An Organizer's Guide to Citizen Action.* New York: Anchor Books.

Gerlach, Luther P. and Hine, Virginia H. (1970) *People, Power, Change: Movements of Social Transformation.* Indianapolis: Bobbs-Merrill.

Gitlin, Todd (2012) *Occupy Nation: The Roots, the Spirit, and the Promise of Occupy Wall Street.* New York: itBooks.

Gladwell, Malcolm (2000) *The Tipping Point: How Little Things Can Make a Big Difference.* Boston: Little, Brown and Company.

Glen, John M. (1988) *Highlander: No Ordinary School, 1932–1962.* Lexington: The University Press of Kentucky.

Goodwin, Lawrence (1978) *The Populist Moment: A Short History of the Agrarian Revolt in America.* Oxford: Oxford University Press.

Gómez-Quiñones, Juan (1990) *Chicano Politics: Reality and Promise, 1940–1990.* Albuquerque: University of New Mexico Press.

169

References

Graeber, David (2000) "Anarchy in the USA." *In These Times*, January 10, pp. 18–19.

Graeber, David (2013) *The Democracy Project: A History, a Crisis, a Movement*. New York: Spiegel & Grau.

Greenberg, Polly (1990) *The Devil Has Slippery Shoes: A Biased Biography of the Child Development Group of Mississippi*. Washington, DC: Youth Policy Institute.

Greenhouse, Steven (2013a) "The workers defense project, a union in spirit." *The New York Times*, August 10. *http://www.nytimes.com/2013/08/11/business/the-workers-defense-project-a-union-in-spirit.html?pagewanted=all&_r=0*. Last accessed May 2, 2014.

Greenhouse, Steven (2013b) "AFL-CIO has plan to add millions of non-union members." *The New York Times*, September 7. *http://www.nytimes.com/2013/09/07/business/afl-cio-has-plan-to-add-millions-of-nonunion-members.html*. Last accessed May 2, 2014.

Halpern, Rick (1997) *Down on the Killing Floor: Black and White Workers in Chicago's Packinghouses, 1904–54*. Urbana and Chicago: University of Illinois Press.

Harrington, Michael (1962) *The Other America: Poverty in the United States*. New York: Macmillan.

Hart, Stephen (2001) *Cultural Dilemmas of Progressive Politics: Styles of Engagement among Grassroots Activists*. Chicago: University of Chicago Press.

Hayden, Tom (2013) *Inspiring Participatory Democracy: Student Movements from Port Huron to Today*. Boulder, CO: Paradigm Publishers.

Healey, Richard and Hinson, Sandra (2005) "Movement strategy for organizers." In David Croteau, William Hoynes, and Charlotte Ryan, eds., *Rhyming Hope and History: Activists, Academics, and Social Movement Scholarship*. Minneapolis: University of Minnesota Press.

Hicks, John D. (1931) *The Populist Revolt: A History of the Farmers' Alliance and the People's Party*. Minneapolis: University of Minnesota Press.

Highlander Research & Education Center (2013) Strategic Assessment and Action, Executive Summary. October. New Market, TN: Highlander Research & Education Center, 8 pp.

Hine, Virginia (1977) "The basic paradigm of a future socio-cultural system." *World Issues*, April/May, pp. 19–22.

Hoffer, Eric (1951) *The True Believer*. New York: Harper & Row (1966 edn).

Hogan, Wesley C. (2007) *Many Minds, One Heart: SNCC's Dream for a New America*. Chapel Hill: University of North Carolina Press.

Horowitz, David (2009) *Barack Obama's Rules for Revolution: The Alinsky Model*. Sherman Oaks, CA: David Horowitz Freedom Center.

Horowitz, David (2010) *The Art of Political War for Tea Parties*. Sherman Oaks, CA: David Horowitz Freedom Center.

References

Horowitz, Roger (1997) *"Negro and White, Unite and Fight": A Social History of Industrial Unionism in Meatpacking, 1930–90*. Urbana: University of Illinois Press.

Horton, Myles (with Kohl, Judith and Kohl, Herbert) (1990) *The Long Haul: An Autobiography*. New York: Doubleday.

Horton, Myles and Freire, Paulo (1990) *We Make the Road by Walking: Conversations on Education and Social Change*. Brenda Bell, John Gaventa, and John Peters, eds. Philadelphia: Temple University Press.

Horwitt, Sanford D. (1989) *Let Them Call Me Rebel: Saul Alinsky – His Life and Legacy*. New York: Alfred A. Knopf.

Hunter, Floyd (1953) *Community Power Structure: A Study of Decision Makers*. Chapel Hill: University of North Carolina Press.

Industrial Areas Foundation (1990) *IAF: 50 Years Organizing for Change*. New York: Industrial Areas Foundation.

Industrial Areas Foundation (1999) *IAF Training Manual*. Chicago: Industrial Areas Foundation.

Isaac, Rael Jean and Isaac, Erich (1985) *The Coercive Utopians: Social Deception by America's Power Players*. Chicago: Regnery Gateway.

Jacobsen, Dennis A. (2001) *Doing Justice: Congregations and Community Organizing*. Minneapolis: Fortress Press.

Johnson, Julie (2011) "Sheriff, SR police recognize Mexico IDs." *The Press Democrat*, October 24, pp. B1–2.

Judis, John B. (2008) "Creation myth." *The New Republic*, September 10, pp. 18–21.

Judis, John B. and Teixeira, Ruy (2004) *The Emerging Democratic Majority*. New York: Scribner.

Karpf, David (2012) *The MoveOn Effect: The Unexpected Transformation of American Political Advocacy*. New York: Oxford University Press.

Katz, Sue (2008–9) "Community organizing is no joke." *Social Policy*, Fall, pp. 13–16.

Katznelson, Ira (2013) *Fear Itself: The New Deal and the Origins of Our Time*. New York: Liveright.

Kazin, Michael (1998) *The Populist Persuasion: An American History*. Revised edn. Ithaca, NY: Cornell University Press.

Kleidman, Robert (2004) "Community organizing and regionalism." *City & Community*, Vol. 3, No. 4, December, pp. 403–20.

Kleidman, Robert (2005) "Congregation-based community organizing and the future of progressive social movements." Paper presented at the 2005 annual meeting of the American Sociological Association.

Klein, Kim (2011) *Fundraising for Social Change*. 6th edn. San Francisco: Jossey-Bass.

Knoepfle, Peg, ed. (1990) *After Alinsky: Community Organizing in Illinois*. Springfield, IL: Sangamon State University.

171

References

Kotz, Nick and Kotz, Mary Lynn (1977) *A Passion for Equality: George A. Wiley and the Movement.* New York: W.W. Norton.

Kretzmann, John P. and McKnight, John L. (1993) *Building Communities from the Inside Out: A Path toward Finding and Mobilizing a Community's Assets.* Skokie, IL: ACTA Publications.

Kurtz, Stanley (2012) *Spreading the Wealth: How Obama Is Robbing the Suburbs to Pay for the Cities.* New York: Penguin.

Laidler, Harry W. (1944) *Social-Economic Movements: An Historical and Comparative Survey of Socialism, Communism, Co-operation, Utopianism, and Other Systems of Reform and Reconstruction.* New York: Thomas Y. Crowell Company.

Larson, Eric, ed. (2013) *Jobs with Justice: 25 years, 25 voices.* Oakland, CA: PM Press.

Le Bon, Gustave (1895) *The Crowd: A Study of the Popular Mind.* New York: Ballantine Books (1969 edn).

Lee, Ntanya and Williams, Steve (2013) *More Than We Imagined: Activists' Assessments on the Moment and the Way Forward.* No place specified: Ear to the Ground Project.

Lemann, Nicholas (1991) *The Promised Land: The Great Black Migration and How It Changed America.* New York: Alfred A. Knopf.

Lipnack, Jessica and Stamps, Jeffrey (1986) *The Networking Book: People Connecting with People.* New York: Routledge & Kegan Paul.

Loeb, Paul Rogat (2004) "The real Rosa Parks." In Paul Rogat Loeb, ed., *The Impossible Will Take a Little While: A Citizen's Guide to Hope in a Time of Fear.* New York: Basic Books.

Luce, Stephanie (2012) "Living wage laws: worth the effort?" *Labor Notes,* No. 396, March.

Lukes, Steven (2005) *Power: A Radical View.* Expanded 2nd edn. New York: Palgrave Macmillan.

Lynd, Alice and Lynd, Staughton, eds. (1973) *Rank and File: Personal Histories by Working-Class Organizers.* Boston: Beacon Press.

McAdam, Doug (1982) *Political Process and the Development of Black Insurgency, 1930–1970.* Chicago: University of Chicago Press.

McCarthy, John D. and Zald, Mayer N. (1973) "The trend of social movements in America." In Mayer N. Zald and John D. McCarthy, eds., *Social Movements in an Organizational Society: Collected Essays.* New Brunswick, NJ: Transaction Publishers, 1987.

MacKay, Charles (1841) *Extraordinary Popular Delusions and the Madness of Crowds.* New York: Harmony Books (1980 edn).

McKnight, John (1995) *The Careless Society: Community and Its Counterfeits.* New York: Basic Books.

McKnight, John and Block, Peter (2012) *The Abundant Community: Awakening the Power of Families and Neighborhoods.* San Francisco: Berrett-Koehler.

References

Mann, Eric (2011) *Playbook for Progressives: 16 Qualities of the Successful Organizer.* Boston: Beacon Press.

Marcus, David (2012) "The horizontalists." *Dissent*, Fall, pp. 54–9.

Marquez, Benjamin (1993) *LULAC: The Evolution of a Mexican American Political Organization.* Austin: University of Texas Press.

Meyerson, Harold (2013) "What divides Democrats." *The American Prospect*, November/December, pp. 44–9.

Michels, Robert (1959) *Political Parties: A Sociological Study of the Oligarchical Tendencies of Modern Democracy.* New York: Dover Publications.

Milkman, Ruth (2012) "Immigrants and the road to power." *Dissent*, Summer, pp. 52–8.

Miller, James (1987) *Democracy Is in the Streets: From Port Huron to the Siege of Chicago.* New York: Simon & Schuster.

Miller, Mike (1987) "Organizing: a map for explorers." *Christianity and Crisis*, February 2, pp. 22–30.

Miller, Mike (1992) "Saul Alinsky and the democratic spirit." *Christianity and Crisis*, No. 52, May 25.

Miller, Mike (1993) "Organizing and education." *Social Policy*, Fall, pp. 51–63.

Miller, Mike (2000) "The lessons of SLATE forty years later: what we did right, what went wrong, how we can overcome." *Social Policy*, Winter, pp. 4–12.

Miller, Mike (2009a) *A Community Organizer's Tale: People and Power in San Francisco.* Berkeley: Heyday Books.

Miller, Mike (2009b) "A critique of John McKnight & John Kretzmann's 'Community Organizing in the Eighties: Toward a Post-Alinsky Agenda.'" *Comm-Org Papers*, Vol. 15.

Miller, Mike (2010) "Alinsky for the left: the politics of community organizing." *Dissent*, Winter, pp. 43–9.

Miller, Mike (2012) *Community Organizing: A Brief Introduction.* Milwaukee: Euclid Avenue Press.

Miller, S.M. (2012) "After the charismatic leader." *Social Policy*, Winter, pp. 53–4.

Mills, C. Wright (1959) *The Power Elite.* New York: Oxford University Press.

Morales, Ricardo Levins and Miller, Mike (2011) "A conversation on building people power for transformative change." *Social Policy*, Vol. 40, No. 4, Winter, pp. 50–3.

Morris, Aldon D. (1984) *The Origins of the Civil Rights Movement: Black Communities Organizing for Change.* New York: Free Press.

Moyer, Bill (2001) *Doing Democracy: The MAP Model for Organizing Social Movements.* Gabriola Island, BC: New Society Publishers.

Moynihan, Daniel P. (1969) *Maximum Feasible Misunderstanding: Community Action in the War on Poverty.* New York: Free Press.

Muñoz, Carlos, Jr. (1989) *Youth, Identity, Power: The Chicano Movement.* London and New York: Verso.

References

National People's Action (n.d. [2013]) *Long-Term Agenda to the New Economy.* Chicago: National People's Action.

Northcott, Kaye (1985) "To agitate the dispossessed . . . : on the road with Ernie Cortes." *Southern Exposure,* July/August, pp. 16–23.

Obama, Barack (1990) "Why organize? Problems and promise in the inner city." In Peg Knoepfle, ed., *After Alinsky: Community Organizing in Illinois.* Springfield, IL: Sangamon State University.

Obama, Barack (1995) *Dreams from My Father: A Story of Race and Inheritance.* New York: Random House.

Obama for America (2008) "Camp Obama deputy field organizer training." San Jose, September 27.

Organizing for America (2009) "Camp Obama volunteer training manual." Northern California, June 13–14.

Parks, Rosa (with Haskins, Jim) (1992) *Rosa Parks: My Story.* New York: Scholastic Inc.

Pastor, Manuel, Perera, Ghan, and Wander, Madeline (2013) *Moments, Movements, and Momentum: Engaging Voters, Scaling Power, Making Change.* Los Angeles: USC Program for Environmental & Regional Equity.

Payne, Charles M. (1995) *I've Got the Light of Freedom: The Organizing Tradition and the Mississippi Freedom Struggle.* Berkeley: University of California Press.

Peace Development Fund (1999) *The Listening Project: A National Dialog on Progressive Movement-Building.* Amherst, MA: Peace Development Fund.

Pfeffer, Paula F. (1990) *A. Philip Randolph, Pioneer of the Civil Rights Movement.* Baton Rouge: Louisiana State University Press.

Pichardo, Nelson A. (1997) "New social movements: a critical review." *Annual Review of Sociology,* pp. 411–30.

Pierce, Gregory F. Augustine (1984) *Activism That Makes Sense: Congregations and Community Organization.* Chicago: ACTA Publications.

Piven, Frances Fox and Cloward, Richard A. (1979) *Poor People's Movements: Why They Succeed, How They Fail.* New York: Vintage Books.

Polletta, Francesca (1994) *Freedom Is an Endless Meeting: Democracy in American Social Movements.* Chicago: University of Chicago Press.

Pollin, Robert and Luce, Stephanie (2000) *The Living Wage: Building a Fair Economy.* New York: The New Press.

Putnam, Robert D. (2000) *Bowling Alone: The Collapse and Revival of American Community.* New York: Simon & Schuster.

Rathke, Wade (2008) "The country roads that created ACORN." In Joe Szakos and Kristin Layng Szakos, eds., *Lessons from the Field: Organizing in Rural Communities.* New Orleans: American Institute for Social Justice/*Social Policy* magazine.

Rathke, Wade (2010) "Spotlight: the United States Social Forum and its window into organizing." *Social Policy,* Fall, pp. 50–1.

References

Rathke, Wade (2011a) "The curious contradictions of community organizing and the United Kingdom." *Social Policy*, Fall, pp. 72–5.

Rathke, Wade (2011b) "Greg Galluzzo of Gamaliel begins to look back." *Social Policy*, Spring, pp. 55–6.

Reitzes, Donald C. and Reitzes, Dietrich C. (1982) "Saul D. Alinsky: a neglected source but promising resource." *The American Sociologist*, Vol. 17, February, pp. 47–56.

Rimer, Sara (2009) "Community organizing never looked so good." *The New York Times*, April 12. *http://www.nytimes.com/2009/04/12/fashion/12organizer. html?pagewanted=all*. Last accessed May 2, 2014.

Robnett, Belinda (1997) *How Long? How Long? African-American Women in the Struggle for Civil Rights*. New York: Oxford University Press.

Rogers, Mary Beth (1990) *Cold Anger: A Story of Faith and Power Politics*. Denton: University of North Texas Press.

Rucht, Dieter (2004) "Movement allies, adversaries, and third parties." In David A. Snow, Sarah A. Soule, and Hanspeter Kriesi, eds., *The Blackwell Companion to Social Movements*. Oxford: Blackwell Publishing.

Rucker, Darnell (1969) *The Chicago Pragmatists*. Minneapolis: University of Minnesota Press.

Rupp, Leila J. and Taylor, Verta (1987) *Survival in the Doldrums: The American Women's Rights Movement, 1945 to the 1960s*. New York: Oxford University Press.

Sale, Kirkpatrick (1994) *SDS*. New York: Random House.

Sanders, Marion K. (1970) *The Professional Radical: Conversations with Saul Alinsky*. New York: Perennial Library.

Schlesinger, Arthur M., Jr. (1986) *The Cycles of American History*. Boston: Houghton Mifflin.

Schneider, Nathan (2013) "Breaking up with Occupy." *The Nation*, September 30, pp. 12–18.

Schrantz, Doran (2013) "Community-based organizing must change. But how?" Rooflines: The Shelterforce Blog, April 3. *http://www.rooflines.org/2908/ community-based_organizing_must_change._but_how/*. Last accessed April 23, 2014.

Schutz, Aaron and Miller, Mike (2014) *People Power: Texts in the Alinsky Organizing Tradition*. Nashville: Vanderbilt University Press.

Schutz, Aaron and Sandy, Marie G. (2011) *Collective Action for Social Change: An Introduction to Community Organizing*. New York: Palgrave Macmillan.

Seltzer, Michael (2002) *Securing Your Organization's Future: A Complete Guide to Fundraising Strategies*. New York: The Foundation Center.

Shirley, Dennis (2002) *Valley Interfaith and School Reform: Organizing for Power in South Texas*. Austin: University of Texas Press.

Silberman, Charles E. (1964) *Crisis in Black and White*. New York: Vintage Books.

References

Skocpol, Theda (2003) *Diminished Democracy: From Membership to Management in American Civic Life*. Norman: University of Oklahoma Press.

Slessarev-Jamir, Helene (2011) *Prophetic Activism: Progressive Religious Justice Movements in Contemporary America*. New York: New York University Press.

Smock, Kristina (2004) *Democracy in Action: Community Organizing and Urban Change*. New York: Columbia University Press.

Smucker, Jonathan Matthew (2012) "Radicals and the 99%: core and mass movement." In Kate Khatib, Margaret Killjoy, and Mike McGuire, eds., *We Are Many: Reflections on Movement Strategy from Occupation to Liberation*. Oakland, CA: AK Press.

Snow, David A. (2004) "Framing processes, ideology, and discursive fields." In David A. Snow, Sarah A. Soule, and Hanspeter Kriesi, eds., *The Blackwell Companion to Social Movements*. Oxford: Blackwell Publishing.

Snow, David A. and Benford, Robert D. (1992) "Master frames and cycles of protest." In Aldon D. Morris and Carol McClurg Mueller, eds., *Frontiers in Social Movement Theory*. New Haven: Yale University Press.

Starhawk (2011) *The Empowerment Manual: A Guide for Collaborative Groups*. Gabriola Island, BC: New Society Publishers.

Stiglitz, Joseph (2011) "Of the 1%, by the 1%, for the 1%." *Vanity Fair*, May. *http://www.vanityfair.com/society/features/2011/05/top-one-percent-201105*. Last accessed May 2, 2014.

Stoecker, Randy (2010) "Has the fight gone out of organizing?" *Shelterforce*, September 2. *http://www.shelterforce.org/article/1983/has_the_fight_gone_out_of_organizing/*. Last accessed May 2, 2014.

Stout, Jeffrey (2010) *Blessed Are the Organized: Grassroots Democracy in America*. Princeton: Princeton University Press.

Swanstrom, Todd and Barrett, Laura (2007) "The road to jobs: the fight for transportation equity." *Social Policy*, Spring/Summer, pp. 76–81.

Swarts, Heidi J. (2008) *Organizing Urban America: Secular and Faith-Based Progressive Movements*. Minneapolis: University of Minnesota Press.

Swarts, Heidi J. (2010) "Organizing nationally to win locally: faith-based community organizing's new frontier." *Shelterforce*, February 12.

Szakos, Joe and Szakos, Kristin Layng, eds. (2008) *Lessons from the Field: Organizing in Rural Communities*. New Orleans: American Institute for Social Justice/*Social Policy* magazine.

Tarrow, Sidney (1994) *Power in Movement: Social Movements, Collective Action and Politics*. Cambridge: Cambridge University Press.

Thornton, J. Mills, III (2002) *Dividing Lines: Municipal Politics and the Struggle for Civil Rights in Montgomery, Birmingham, and Selma*. Tuscaloosa: University of Alabama Press.

Thucydides (1954) *History of the Peloponnesian War*. Trans. Rex Warner. Intro. M.I. Finley. London: Penguin Books.

References

Tilly, Charles (2004) *Social Movements, 1768–2001*. Boulder, CO: Paradigm Publishers.

Trapp, Shel (1976) *A Challenge for Change*. Chicago: National Training and Information Center.

Trapp, Shel (1979) *Who, Me a Researcher? Yes You!* Chicago: National Training and Information Center.

Trapp, Shel (1986) *Basics of Organizing*. Chicago: National Training and Information Center.

von Drehle, David (2003) *Triangle: The Fire That Changed America*. New York: Atlantic Monthly Press.

von Hoffman, Nicholas (n.d.) "Finding and making leaders." Handout, 10 pp.

von Hoffman, Nicholas (2010) *Radical: A Portrait of Saul Alinsky*. New York: Nation Books.

Walker, Edward and McCarthy, John (2012) "Continuity and change in community organizing." *Social Policy*, Summer, pp. 3–7.

Walls, David (1980) Review of Frances Fox Piven and Richard A. Cloward, *Poor People's Movements: Why They Succeed, How They Fail*. *Rural Sociology*, Vol. 45, Spring, pp. 171–3.

Walls, David (1993) *The Activist's Almanac: The Concerned Citizen's Guide to the Leading Advocacy Organizations in America*. New York: Simon & Schuster/ Fireside.

Walls, David (2009–10) "Review essay: the Appalachian Volunteers in perspective." *Appalachian Journal*, Vol. 37, Nos. 1–2, Fall/Winter, pp. 100–5.

Walls, David (2011) "Action, scholarship, reflection, renewal." *Journal of Appalachian Studies*, Vol. 17, Nos. 1–2, Spring/Fall, pp. 9–15, 23–5.

Walls, David (2012) "Relational organizing or therapeutic politics?" in "Symposium: organizing and therapeutic politics." *Dissent Magazine Online*, October 18. *http://www.dissentmagazine.org/online_articles/symposium-organizing-and-therapeutic-politics#walls*. Last accessed April 23, 2014.

Walls, David and Stephenson, John B., eds. (1972) *Appalachia in the Sixties: Decade of Reawakening*. Lexington: University Press of Kentucky.

Walton, Mary (2010) *A Woman's Crusade: Alice Paul and the Battle for the Ballot*. New York: Palgrave Macmillan.

Warren, Mark R. (2001) *Dry Bones Rattling: Community Building to Revitalize American Democracy*. Princeton: Princeton University Press.

Weber, Max (1946) "Politics as a vocation." In *From Max Weber: Essays in Sociology*. H.H. Gerth and C. Wright Mills, eds. New York: Oxford University Press.

Weiner, Rachel (2013) "MoveOn.org moving to petition-driven model." *The Washington Post*, March 15. *http://www.washingtonpost.com/blogs/post-politics/wp/2013/03/15/moveon-org-moving-to-petition-driven-model/*. Last accessed May 2, 2014.

References

Wellstone, Paul David (1978) *How the Rural Poor Got Power: Narrative of a Grass-Roots Organizer.* Amherst: University of Massachusetts Press.

Westgate, Michael (with Vick-Westgate, Ann) (2011) *Gale Force: Gale Cincotta, the Battles for Disclosure and Community Reinvestment.* Cambridge, MA: Harvard Bookstore.

Whitman, Gordon (2006–7) "Beyond advocacy: the history and vision of the PICO Network." *Social Policy*, Winter, pp. 50–9.

Whitman, Gordon (2009) "What happens when people speak about health care." *Social Policy*, Spring, pp. 21–31.

Wilkinson, M. James (2010) *Who Rules Santa Rosa and Why It Matters.* New York: iUniverse Inc.

Wills, Gary (1994a) "What makes a good leader?" *The Atlantic Monthly*, April, pp. 63–71.

Wills, Gary (1994b) *Certain Trumpets: The Nature of Leadership.* New York: Simon & Schuster.

Wood, Richard L. (2002) *Faith in Action: Religion, Race and Democratic Organizing in America.* Chicago: University of Chicago Press.

Wood, Richard L., Fulton, Brad, and Partridge, Kathryn (2013) *Building Bridges, Building Power: Developments in Institution-Based Community Organizing.* New York: Interfaith Funders.

Zald, Mayer N. and McCarthy, John D., eds. (1987) *Social Movements in an Organizational Society: Collected Essays.* New Brunswick, NJ: Transaction Publishers.

Index

Index

Index

Index

power
  analysis, 78–80
  described, 60–1
prefigurative politics, 135
President's Commission on the Status
  of Women, 133
Price, Gregory, 66
progressivism, 16–17
public meetings, 85–7
Putnam, Robert, 43

Queens Citizens Organization, 51

Randolph, A. Philip
  and E.D. Nixon, 79–80
  on organizing, 77
  wins demands from FDR and
  Truman,114–16
Rathke, Dale, 107–8
Rathke, Wade, 105–8, 137, 154
resource mobilization, 10–11
Rerum Novarum, 50
Reveille for Radicals (Alinsky), 28–9
Reynolds, David, 153
Robinson, Jo Ann Gibson, 57
Robnett, Belinda, 66–7
Roots for Radicals (Chambers), 42
Ross, Fred, 29–32, 35
Rothstein, Richard, 143
Roybal, Edward, 30–1
Rules for Radicals (Alinsky), 38–40
Rusk, David, 99

Sandy, Marie, 64
Schrantz, Doran, 6
Schutz, Aaron
  on self-interest, 64
  on tactics, 104–5
Schwartzhaupt Foundation, 31, 33
SDS, *see* Students for a Democratic
  Society ’
Shaw, Clifford, 24, 26
Shaw, Susan, 72

Sheil, Bishop Bernard J., 26
Sherman, Gordon, 37
Shirley, Dennis, 44
Sinclair, Upton, 25
Smock, Kristina, 125–6, 135, 143,
  151
Smucker, Jonathan Matthew, 195–6
SNCC, *see* Student Nonviolent
  Coordinating Committee
social constructionism, 12
social movement
  analysis, 9–13
  definition, 7
  typology, 8–9
Southern Christian Leadership
  Conference (SCLC), 10, 34
Southwest Voter Registration
  Education Project, 45
SPIN model, 92–5
Starhawk, 143
Starr, Vicki, 26
Stephens, Sister Christine, 66, 75
strategic analysis, 82
strategic planning, 80–1
strategy, 65, 115–18
Student Nonviolent Coordinating
  Committee (SNCC), 10, 37,
  132
Students for a Democratic Society
  (SDS), 37, 104, 132
Swarts, Heidi, 8–9

Thucydides, 62–3
Tilly, Charles, 73, 87
Tjerandsen, Carl, 31
Transportation Equity Network
  (TEN), 100
Trapp, Shel
  interview, 161
  and NPA, 102–3
  on negotiation, 76–7
  on research, 74
Trumka, Richard, 152–3